TRACKED
FIREPOWER

TODAY'S ARMORED FIGHTING VEHICLES

TRACKED
FIREPOWER

TODAY'S ARMORED FIGHTING VEHICLES

Jason Turner

MBI Publishing Company

This edition first published in 2002 by MBI Publishing Company, Galtier Plaza, Suite 200
380 Jackson Street, St. Paul, MN 55101-3885 USA

MBI Publishing Company books are also available at discounts in bulk quantity for industrial or sales-promotional use. For details write to Special Sales Manager at Motorbooks International Wholesalers & Distributors, Galtier Plaza, Suite 200, 380 Jackson Street, St. Paul, MN 55101-3885 USA

ISBN 0-7603-1410-1

Printed in Hong Kong

Editor: Claire Chandler
Picture research: Andrew Webb
Design: Iain Stewart
Production: Matt Weyland

CONTENTS

SK 105

Steyr-Daimler-Puch Spezialfahrzeug AG & Co KG developed the SK 105 light tank, known as the *Kurassier*, to meet the Austrian Army's operational requirement for a mobile anti-tank vehicle. Although classified as "tank destroyer" (*Jagdpanzer*) by the Austrian Army, it is considered a light tank. The first pre-production vehicles were completed in 1971, and since then almost 700 have been built for home and export markets. The SK 105 shares many common automotive components with the Steyr fully tracked armoured personnel carrier. It is fitted with a two-man oscillating turret armed with a 105mm rifled gun, which is fed by two revolver-type magazines, each of which holds six rounds. The empty cartridge cases are ejected outside of the turret bustle at the rear. The SK 105 has been constantly improved, and the latest production version features a computerized fire control system with day/night sights for the commander and gunner and a new fully automatic transmission. Options for the SK 105 include an upgrade package to bring older vehicles up to the latest production standard, NBC (nuclear, biological, chemical) protection system and new night-vision equipment. Many of its automotive components are identical to those used in the armoured troop carrier vehicles built by Steyr.

SPECIFICATIONS

Type:	*light tank*
Crew:	*3*
Weight:	*17,500kg (38,500lb)*
Length (Gun Forward):	*7.76m (25.45ft)*
Height:	*2.88m (9.44ft)*
Width:	*2.5m (8.2ft)*
Ground Clearance:	*0.4m (1.3ft)*
Vertical Obstacle:	*0.8m (2.62ft)*
Trench:	*2.4m (7.87ft)*
Gradient:	*75 percent*
Powerplant:	*Steyr 7FA diesel*
Power Rating:	*320hp*
Speed – Maximum:	*68km/h (42.5mph)*
Cruising Range:	*520km (325 miles)*
Main Armament:	*1 x 105mm*
Secondary Armament:	*2 x 7.62mm*
Ammunition:	*41 x 105mm, 2000 x 7.62mm*

TYPE 85

The Type 85 tank is a modification of the earlier Type 80, which was in turn based on the Soviet T-54, with an improved turret changed from a cast design to a welded variant. The newest model, the Type 85-III, incorporates features also found in the newer Type 90 tank, including a larger 125mm smoothbore main gun capable of firing armour-piercing, fin-stabilized, discarding sabot (APFSDS), high-explosive, anti-tank (HEAT) and high-explosive, anti-tank fragmentation (HEAT-FRAG) rounds. The more recent BK-27 HEAT round offers increased penetration against conventional armour and explosive reactive armour (ERA). The BK-29 round, with a hard penetrator in the nose, is designed for use against reactive armour and also has fragmentation effects. A stabilized image intensification sight allows the Type 85 to engage moving targets while in motion. A GEC-Marconi Centaur fire control system is also available, while the British Barr and Stroud thermal-based fire control system can be fitted. The Type 85-III uses modular composite armour, and some reports suggest the incorporation of reactive armour. Composite panels are available to improve protection, while the crew can achieve a rate of fire of up to six rounds per minute, though it is customary for crews to halt before firing.

SPECIFICATIONS

Type:	main battle tank
Crew:	3
Weight:	41,000kg (90,200lb)
Length (Gun Forward):	10.28m (33.72ft)
Height:	2.3m (7.54ft)
Width:	3.45m (11.31ft)
Ground Clearance:	0.48m (1.57ft)
Vertical Obstacle:	0.8m (2.62ft)
Trench:	2.7m (8.85ft)
Gradient:	60 percent
Powerplant:	V-12 supercharged diesel
Power Rating:	730hp
Speed – Maximum:	57.25km/h (35.78mph)
Cruising Range:	500km (312 miles)
Main Armament:	1 x 125mm
Secondary Armament:	1 x 7.62mm , 1 x 12.7mm
Ammunition:	40 x 125mm, 2000 x 7.62mm

TYPE 90

The Type 90 incorporates significant improvements over the Type 85, including modular composite armour, a stabilized turret, slaved targeting sight and gun, passive thermal imaging, and an autoloading, smoothbore 125mm gun capable of firing armour-piercing, fin-stabilized, discarding sabot (APFSDS), high-explosive, anti-tank (HEAT) and high-explosive, anti-tank fragmentation (HEAT-FRAG) rounds. A family of explosive reactive armour (ERA) systems has been developed by China North Industries Corporation (NORINCO). The armour improves survivability against high-explosive, anti-tank (HEAT), kinetic energy and tandem HEAT projectiles. With the addition of reactive armour panels, an improved laser rangefinder and increased mobility, the Type 90-II is currently the most advanced Chinese main battle tank. Although not yet in service in large quantities, it is known that the People's Liberation Army (PLA) ordered 00 Type 90-IIs, without advanced fire control systems, in 1999. China, following Russian tradition, has mounted anti-tank guided weapons on its tanks, and the latest is the Red Arrow 9 anti-tank guided weapon (ATGW). The Type 90 should enter service in large numbers, but given the fragile state of China's finances, it is not known how many Type 90s will ultimately be built.

SPECIFICATIONS

Type:	*main battle tank*
Crew:	*3*
Weight:	*43,636kg (96,000lb)*
Length (Gun Forward):	*10.28m (33.72ft)*
Height:	*2.3m (7.54ft)*
Width:	*3.45m (11.31ft)*
Ground Clearance:	*0.48m (1.57ft)*
Vertical Obstacle:	*0.8m (2.62ft)*
Trench:	*2.7m (8.85ft)*
Gradient:	*60 percent*
Powerplant:	*8-cylinder turbocharged diesel*
Power Rating:	*1200hp*
Speed – Maximum:	*59km/h (37mph)*
Cruising Range:	*unknown*
Main Armament:	*1 x 125mm*
Secondary Armament:	*1 x 12.7mm, 1 x 7.62mm*
Ammunition:	*unknown*

ADATS

ADATS (Air Defence Anti-Tank System) is one of the world's premier low-level air defence systems. It uses pulse-Doppler radar and electro-optics to detect targets and engage them with accurate laser beam-rider guided missiles. ADATS employs an integrated command, control and communications (C3) network that can coordinate the firepower of up to six ADATS systems. The ADATS system itself is highly mobile. For example, it can be mounted on a variety of mobile platforms such as the M113 and M3 Bradley vehicles. The system includes a fully automatic real-time data exchange with airspace control data, weapon control orders and fire control orders, target identification data, individual system status and vehicle position, threat prioritization and optimized weapon allocation. A six-unit ADATS network can engage up to 48 air or ground targets simultaneously. Initial target detection to missile launch takes less than five seconds. The tracker search and target acquisition sequence is carried out using the forward-looking infrared (FLIR) and the television sighting system. Missile launch and guidance uses FLIR and television target tracking and carbon dioxide laser beam-riding missile guidance. The time required to launch a second missile following completion of the first engagement is less than two seconds.

SPECIFICATIONS

Type:	*self-propelled SAM*
Crew:	*3*
Weight:	*22,940kg (50,468lb)*
Length:	*6.55 m (21.48ft)*
Height:	*2.97m (9.74ft)*
Width:	*3.61m (11.84ft)*
Ground Clearance:	*0.43m (1.41ft)*
Vertical Obstacle:	*0.91m (2.98ft)*
Trench:	*2.54m (8.33ft)*
Gradient:	*60 percent*
Powerplant:	*VTA-903T turbocharged diesel*
Power Rating:	*500hp*
Speed – Maximum:	*60km/h (37.5mph)*
Cruising Range:	*483km (302 miles)*
Main Armament:	*8 ready-to-fire SAMs*
Secondary Armament:	*none*
Ammunition:	*8 x SAM*

CV 90

The Combat Vehicle 90 (CV 90) is jointly developed and manufactured by Hägglunds AB (chassis) and Bofors AB (turret, armament and ammunition). The CV 90 family consists of a number of variants: CV 90 (the basic armoured infantry fighting vehicle, armed with a 30mm automatic cannon); anti-aircraft vehicle 90; forward observer vehicle 90; command post vehicle 90; and recovery vehicle 90. All are designed for use in inhospitable terrain and hostile combat environments. The CV 90 is an extremely agile, multirole combat vehicle with all-target capability, a low, very compact structure and minimized radar and infrared signatures. The basic turret is electrically operated and houses a sight with integrated laser rangefinder and thermal camera. The 30mm cannon can knock out all other light armoured vehicles and even offers a chance to kill enemy tanks from flanking positions. A total of 500 CV 90s have been procured for the Swedish Army, with final delivery taking place in 2002. The Hägglunds Vehicle CV 90120 light tank consists of a slightly modified CV 90 chassis, produced for both Norway and Sweden, and fitted with a new three-man turret mounting a Swiss Ordnance 120mm smoothbore gun with a computerized fire control system and stabilized day/night sights.

SPECIFICATIONS

Type:	*infantry fighting vehicle*
Crew:	*3 + 8*
Weight:	*26,000kg (57,200lb)*
Length:	*6.54m (21.45ft)*
Height:	*2.73m (8.95ft)*
Width:	*3.19m (10.46ft)*
Ground Clearance:	*0.45m (1.47ft)*
Vertical Obstacle:	*1.2m (3.93ft)*
Trench:	*2.4m (7.87ft)*
Gradient:	*60 percent*
Powerplant:	*Scania DSI 14 diesel*
Power Rating:	*605hp*
Speed – Maximum:	*70km/h (43.75mph)*
Cruising Range:	*unknown*
Main Armament:	*1 x 30mm*
Secondary Armament:	*1 x 7.62mm*
Ammunition:	*400 x 30mm, 3800 x 7.62mm*

TAM

The TAM (*Tanque Argentino Mediano* – Argentine Medium Tank) is a military vehicle based on the German Marder 1 infantry vehicle. The main differences include different powerpacks and slightly heavier armour for the tank version. The TAM and the infantry version, the VCTP (*Vehiculo de Combate Transporte de Personal –* Combat Vehicle Personnel Transport), were shown as prototypes in the mid-1970s and are now the standard equipment of Argentine Army mechanized units. A family of derivative vehicles in various stages of development include the VCPM mortar carrier, VCRC recovery vehicle, VCTC command vehicle, VCLC rocket launcher, and a self-propelled howitzer carrying a locally produced version of the Italian Palmaria gun. The first few TAMs were equipped with the locally produced variant of the L7A1 gun. Later vehicles were armed with the Rheinmetall LTA2, and the last produced vehicles were equipped with a locally produced modified version of the French CN-105-57, produced in the TAMSE military factory of Rio Tercero, in Cordoba province. The TAM is also equipped with two smoke grenade launchers, with each launcher firing four grenades. In addition, the vehicle is NBC proof and can be fitted with a night-vision system.

SPECIFICATIONS

Type:	*medium tank*
Crew:	*4*
Weight:	*30,000kg (66,000lb)*
Length (Gun Forward):	*8.23m (27ft)*
Height:	*2.43m (7.97ft)*
Width:	*3.29m (10.79ft)*
Ground Clearance:	*0.45m (1.47ft)*
Vertical Obstacle:	*1m (3.28ft)*
Trench:	*2.5m (8.2ft)*
Gradient:	*60 percent*
Powerplant:	*MTU MB 833 Ka 500 diesel*
Power Rating:	*720hp*
Speed – Maximum:	*75km/h (46.87mph)*
Cruising Range:	*550km (344 miles)*
Main Armament:	*1 x 105mm*
Secondary Armament:	*1 x 7.62mm*
Ammunition:	*50 x 105mm, 6000 x 7.62mm*

AMX-10P

The AMX-10P is the support and freight vehicle of the mechanized infantry units, and it carries squadrons of the combat regiments. This tracked amphibious armoured vehicle transports a group of nine men in addition to the driver and gunner under the turret. It has a great autonomy and excellent terrestrial and water mobility which allows it, in particular, to cross by its own means a flooded cut. Its 20mm gun enables it to engage light armoured tanks and even low-flying aircraft. Protected against weapons of average gauge and the shrapnel of artillery shells, it can also fight in an NBC environment. A French SNPE explosive reactive armour (ERA) kit is available for use on the AMX-10P. However, during combat ERA would be a hazard to dismounting troops and so passive armour is preferable. There are a number of variants of this vehicle: the basic AMX-10P with Milan or HOT anti-tank guided missiles (ATGMs) – AMX-10P/Milan; AMX-10 PAC 90, a fire support/anti-tank variant with a Giat 90mm gun; AMX-10P Marine, an improved amphibious variant with a 12.7mm, 25mm or 90mm gun; AMX-10 PC, a command variant with varied command stations; AMX-10 RC, a wheeled (6 x 6) fire support vehicle armed with a 90mm gun; and AMX-10 RAC, the same fire support chassis with a 105mm gun.

SPECIFICATIONS

Type:	infantry combat vehicle
Crew:	2 + 9
Weight:	14,500kg (31,900lb)
Length:	5.75m (18.86ft)
Height:	2.57m (8.43ft)
Width:	2.78m (9.12ft)
Ground Clearance:	0.45m (1.47ft)
Vertical Obstacle:	0.7m (2.2ft)
Trench:	2.1m (6.88ft)
Gradient:	60 percent
Powerplant:	Scania DSI 14 diesel
Power Rating:	300hp
Speed – Maximum:	70km/h (43.75mph)
Cruising Range:	600km (375 miles)
Main Armament:	1 x 20mm
Secondary Armament:	1 x 7.62mm
Ammunition:	800 x 20mm, 2000 x 7.62mm

AMX-13

Design work on the AMX-13 light tank began in 1946 at the Atelier de Construction d'Issy-les-Moulineaux and the first prototype was completed two years later. Production was undertaken at the Atelier de Construction Roanne (ARE) from 1952, with the first production tanks completed the following year. At one time production of the tank was running at 45 units per month but in the early 1960s production of the whole family was transferred to the civilian company of Creusot-Loire at Chalon sur Saône as the ARE was tooling up for production of the AMX-30. The basic AMX-13 chassis has been used for a wide range of vehicles, including self-propelled guns and anti-aircraft systems. Improvements include a new power-pack consisting of a diesel engine coupled to a fully automatic transmission and the replacement of the torsion bar suspension by a new hydropneumatic suspension for improved cross-country mobility. The AMX-13 is no longer being marketed by Giat Industries. It is estimated that total production of the AMX-13 family of light tracked vehicles, including the light tank, amounted to 7700 units, of which around 3400 were exported. The AMX-13 tank was phased out of service with the French Army many years ago, but it is still in use in the developing world.

SPECIFICATIONS

Type:	*light tank*
Crew:	*3*
Weight:	*15,000kg (33,000lb)*
Length (Gun Forward):	*6.36m (20.86ft)*
Height:	*2.3m (7.54ft)*
Width:	*2.51m (8.23ft)*
Ground Clearance:	*0.37m (1.21ft)*
Vertical Obstacle:	*0.65m (2.13ft)*
Trench:	*1.6m (5.24ft)*
Gradient:	*60 percent*
Powerplant:	*SOFAM Model 8 petrol*
Power Rating:	*250hp*
Speed – Maximum:	*60km/h (37.5mph)*
Cruising Range:	*400km (250 miles)*
Main Armament:	*1 x 90mm*
Secondary Armament:	*2 x 7.62mm*
Ammunition:	*32 x 90mm, 3600 x 7.62mm*

AMX-30

Giat Industries has built and delivered to a dozen armies almost 2300 AMX-30 main battle tanks, as well as 1100 derivative versions (155 GCT self-propelled howitzers, anti-aircraft missile or gun systems and armoured recovery vehicles). The AMX-30 B2 is an improved version of the tank, achieved either by rebuilding existing models or by production of new tanks, and is equipped with an automatic fire control system. The AMX-30 is well profiled, strongly armed, equipped with very good mobility and a great autonomy. It is encased in rolled plates and castings, entirely welded and has a cast turret. Its lack of composite armour puts it at a distinct disadvantage in tank-versus-tank engagements. In reality, it is protected only from small-gauge weapons and the effects of artillery. The AMX-30 B2 is able to fight in an NBC environment and to cross water up to 2m (6.5ft) deep (4m [13.12ft] with a snorkel). It is intended for all missions requiring operations by traditional armoured forces: the direct destruction of the enemy forces, and the immediate exploitation of break-throughs achieved by other weapon systems, including the battlefield deployment of nuclear weapons. The AMX-30 is now no longer in French frontline service, having been replaced by the Leclerc.

SPECIFICATIONS

Type:	*main battle tank*
Crew:	*4*
Weight:	*36,000kg (79,200lb)*
Length (Gun Forward):	*9.48m (31.1ft)*
Height:	*2.85m (9.35ft)*
Width:	*3.1m (10.17ft)*
Ground Clearance:	*0.44m (1.44ft)*
Vertical Obstacle:	*0.93m (3.05ft)*
Trench:	*2.9m (9.51ft)*
Gradient:	*60 percent*
Powerplant:	*Hispano-Suiza HS 110*
Power Rating:	*720hp*
Speed – Maximum:	*65km/h (40.62mph)*
Cruising Range:	*600km (375 miles)*
Main Armament:	*1 x 105mm*
Secondary Armament:	*1 x 20mm, 1 x 7.62mm*
Ammunition:	*47 x 105mm, 1050 x 20mm*

AUF-1

This 155mm self-propelled howitzer is intended to equip forces with armoured artillery to provide direct and indirect fire. The 155mm gun is assembled from a turret on the chassis of the AMX-30, providing mobility close to that of the main battle tank. The gun's range is 23.5km (14.68 miles) with normal ammunition and 30km (18.75 miles) with long-range ammunition. Normal ammunition is a high-explosive shell with a hollow base. The initial speed in maximum loading is 810 metres pre second (2657 feet per second). The vehicle is capable of carrying 42 complete rounds: 7 racks of 6 shells, 7 racks of 6 combustible casings. Re-stocking of ammunition can be achieved in 15 minutes with 4 men. The pace of firing with an automatic attachment feeding in ammunition, using combustible casings, allows the gun to fire 6 shots in 45 seconds and 12 shots in 2 minutes. In the event of a partial or total breakdown of this device, firing is still possible manually but at reduced rate. The vehicle can operate on an NBC battlefield due to the sealing of the turret, and the crew is also protected from the projectiles of light automatic weapons. The secondary armament is a 12.7mm machine gun, which provides some defence against aircraft and enemy infantry. The AUF-1 was used by Coalition forces in the 1991 Gulf War.

SPECIFICATIONS

Type:	*self-propelled howitzer*
Crew:	*4*
Weight:	*42,000kg (92,400lb)*
Length (Gun Forward):	*10.25m (33.62ft)*
Height:	*3.25m (10.66ft)*
Width:	*3.15m (10.33ft)*
Ground Clearance:	*0.42m (1.37ft)*
Vertical Obstacle:	*0.93m (3.05ft)*
Trench:	*1.9m (6.23ft)*
Gradient:	*60 percent*
Powerplant:	*Hispano-Suiza HS 110*
Power Rating:	*720hp*
Speed – Maximum:	*60km/h (37.5mph)*
Cruising Range:	*450km (281 miles)*
Main Armament:	*1 x 155mm*
Secondary Armament:	*1 x 12.7mm*
Ammunition:	*42 x 155mm, 800 x 12.7mm*

CROTALE

rotale is an all-weather, short-range air defence system whose mission is the defence of frontline armoured brigades, permanent or semi-permanent site defence, and area defence against air threats: fixed-wing aircraft, attack helicopters, cruise missiles, tactical missiles and saturation attacks with stand-off weapons released from aircraft and helicopters. The Crotale system provides air situation and threat assessment, extended detection range, identification friend-or-foe (IFF), multi-target detection plus automated acquisition, and tracking and engagement. The latest version Crotale Next Generation (NG) entered production in 1990 and is in service with the Finnish Army (20 systems), the French Air Force (12 shelter-mounted systems) and the French Navy. The manufacturer, Thales Optronics, signed a contract with Greece in June 1999 for 11 Crotale NG systems: nine for the Air Force and two for the Navy. It has also been sold to Saudi Arabia and Oman. The system is equipped with a multi-sensor suite including passive electro-optics and radar with built-in electronic counter countermeasures (ECCM) to engage airborne targets under adverse conditions of dense electronic warfare and hostile battlefield environments, including NBC and smoke and dust screens.

SPECIFICATIONS

Type:	self-propelled SAM
Crew:	3
Weight:	18,182kg (40,000lb)
Length:	4.86m (16ft)
Height:	2.68m (8.79ft)
Width:	2.68m (8.79ft)
Ground Clearance:	0.43m (1.41ft)
Vertical Obstacle:	0.61m (2ft)
Trench:	2.18m (7.15ft)
Gradient:	60 percent
Powerplant:	Detroit Diesel 6V53TIA
Power Rating:	400hp
Speed – Maximum:	66km/h (41mph)
Cruising Range:	480km (300 miles)
Main Armament:	8 x Crotale NG VT1 missiles
Secondary Armament:	none
Ammunition:	Crotale NG VT1 missiles

LECLERC

The Leclerc was designed to be highly capable in combat against all potential enemy tanks in day or night at ranges in excess of 3000m (9842ft). It includes a gun with an automatic loading system which makes it possible to quickly select the type of ammunition, and is capable of firing when the tank is moving and can achieve a rate of fire of up to six shots per minute. The long-range fire control system stabilizes the sight, keeping the gun permanently pointed at the target. There are two sights: one for the commander of the tank and the other for the operator. The turret acquires the target with gyro-stabilizers, and a video re-copy of the images allows sharing of information between the two. Unequalled mobility is obtained by the synergy between the motor, the kinematic chain, and the hydropneumatic suspension. A very balanced general protection is obtained not only by modular shieldings but also by compactness and thus low visibility, which, combined with the very great agility of the tank, makes it a difficult target to hit. Onboard, tactical or logistic decisions are made easier by the digitalization of all data. The radio operator station makes it possible to coordinate the whole of the armoured battle group by the use of the system of control and command installed on board the Leclerc.

SPECIFICATIONS

Type:	*main battle tank*
Crew:	*3*
Weight:	*54,500kg (119,900lb)*
Length (Gun Forward):	*9.87m (32.38ft)*
Height:	*2.53m (8.3ft)*
Width:	*3.71m (12.17ft)*
Ground Clearance:	*0.5m (1.64ft)*
Vertical Obstacle:	*1.25m (4.1ft)*
Trench:	*3m (9.84ft)*
Gradient:	*60 percent*
Powerplant:	*SACM V8X diesel*
Power Rating:	*1500hp*
Speed – Maximum:	*71km/h (44.3mph)*
Cruising Range:	*550km (344 miles)*
Main Armament:	*1 x 120mm*
Secondary Armament:	*2 x 12.7mm*
Ammunition:	*40 x 120mm*

ROLAND 2

The Roland 2 weapon system is intended for the anti-aircraft defence of armoured and mechanized units to counter aircraft flying to nearly Mach 1.5 and hovering helicopters. Roland is generally employed either in complement of the coverage of the American Hawk system's defence of zones and corridors not defended by the latter, or as an extension of the Hawk system itself. The Hawk missile is a surface-to-air missile (SAM) system that provides medium-range air defence against both aircraft and missiles. Roland ensures the overall defence of a zone of 100 square kilometres (62.5 square miles) against a threat posed by a flight of four aircraft or two flights acting at more than 20-second intervals. Deployed on a tracked vehicle derived from the AMX-30 main battle tank, it comprises a radar with a range of 16km (10 miles), a sighting tube with an infrared locator that measures the difference between the missile in flight and the line of sight of the fire control radar, and a computer antenna for remote control. The target is detected by the radar, and the continuation of the target after acquisition is carried out manually in radar mode. Roland has a reload time of around 10 seconds, though this may increase in a battlefield environment. The missiles themselves have an altitude of 5500m (16,404ft).

SPECIFICATIONS

Type:	*self-propelled SAM*
Crew:	*3*
Weight:	*32,500kg (71,500kg)*
Length:	*6.91m (22.67ft)*
Height:	*2.92m (9.58ft)*
Width:	*3.24m (10.62ft)*
Ground Clearance:	*0.44m (1.44ft)*
Vertical Obstacle:	*1.15m (3.72ft)*
Trench:	*2.5m (8.2ft)*
Gradient:	*60 percent*
Powerplant:	*MTU MB 833 Ea 500 diesel*
Power Rating:	*600hp*
Speed – Maximum:	*70km/h (43.75mph)*
Cruising Range:	*520km (325 miles)*
Main Armament:	*2 x Roland SAM*
Secondary Armament:	*1 x 7.62mm*
Ammunition:	*8 x Roland SAM*

ASRAD

The light mechanized Short-Range Air Defence System (SHORAD) has been developed for the German Army by STN ATLAS Elektronik GmbH in Bremen and Krauss-Maffei Wegmann (KMW) in Kassel, Germany. The export version is known as the Atlas Short-Range Air Defence System (ASRAD). It is based on the Wiesel 2 carrier vehicle and provides protection for vital assets such as command, control, communications and information centres (C3I centres), airfields and troops on the move, or on the battlefield against the threat of low-level fixed-wing and rotary wing aircraft. ASRAD carries four ready-to-fire surface-to-air missiles (SAMs), including the Stinger, Igla, the RBS 70 Mk 2 and others. It is air transportable in a CH-53 helicopter. Target acquisition is achieved either by the 3-D HARD radar installed on the platoon command post, which downloads target data via radio data link to the vehicle, or by the Pilkington Optronics Air Defence Alerting Device (ADAD) passive infrared search and track system (IRST), mounted on the forward part of the roof. For target tracking, the vehicle is equipped with its own stabilized forward-looking infrared (FLIR) sensor, TV and laser rangefinder as well as dual mode auto-tracking. The vehicle is lightweight, making it ideal for use with rapid-reaction and airborne forces.

SPECIFICATIONS

Type:	*self-propelled SAM*
Crew:	*3*
Weight:	*2800kg (6160kg)*
Length:	*3.31m (10.85ft)*
Height:	*2m (6.56ft)*
Width:	*1.82m (5.97ft)*
Ground Clearance:	*0.3m (0.98ft)*
Vertical Obstacle:	*0.4m (1.13ft)*
Trench:	*1.2m (3.93ft)*
Gradient:	*60 percent*
Powerplant:	*VW turbocharged diesel*
Power Rating:	*86hp*
Speed – Maximum:	*75km/h (46.87mph)*
Cruising Range:	*300km (188 miles)*
Main Armament:	*4 x SAM*
Secondary Armament:	*none*
Ammunition: `	*unknown*

GEPARD

The vehicle is fitted with a fire control system, all-weather tracking, acquisition sensors and powerful automatic guns. Its role is to protect key installations, combat units and troops on the move and on the battlefield. Gepard is fitted with a two-man electric-operated turret armed with twin Oerlikon KDA 35mm guns, which have automatic belt feed. The rate of fire provided by the two barrels is 1100 rounds per minute, and each gun has 320 rounds of ready-to-fire anti-air ammunition and 20 rounds of anti-ground target ammunition. The guns are capable of firing a range of standardized 35mm ammunition including the latest frangible armour-piercing, discarding sabot (FAPDS) round, which has a muzzle velocity over 1400 mps (4593fps). The Gepard is equipped with eight smoke dischargers installed on either side of the turret for protection, and future plans include fitting the Stinger surface-to-air missile (SAM) system, whose launching system will be fitted on the side of the 35mm twin guns. Gepard is equipped with independent search and tracking radars, the search radar installed at the front rear of the turret and the tracking radar on the rear front of the turret. The radars provide 360-degree scanning with simultaneous target tracking, clutter suppression and search-on-the-move capability.

SPECIFICATIONS

Type:	self-propelled anti-aircraft gun
Crew:	3
Weight:	47,300kg (104,060lb)
Length (Gun Forward):	7.73m (25.36ft)
Height:	4.03m (13.22ft)
Width:	3.71m (12.17ft)
Ground Clearance:	0.5m (1.64ft)
Vertical Obstacle:	1.15m (3.77ft)
Trench:	3m (9.84ft)
Gradient:	60 percent
Powerplant:	Type OM314 diesel
Power Rating:	830hp
Speed – Maximum:	65km/h (40.62mph)
Cruising Range:	550km (344 miles)
Main Armament:	2 x 35mm
Secondary Armament:	none
Ammunition:	320 (AA) & 20 (AP) per gun

JAGUAR

The *Jagdpanzer Rakete* was a modern tank destroyer and featured the SS-11 missile. There were 370 built in 1967–68, and they shared the same chassis with the now-defunct *Jagdpanzer Kanone* 90mm self-propelled anti-tank gun. Between 1978 and 1983 316 of the original *Raketen* were rebuilt and their missiles upgraded to the more advanced Euromissile K3S ATGW. The armour on the front and sides was upgraded with appliqué packages to improve protection against HEAT warheads. These rebuilt vehicles were designated Jaguar 1s. Between 1983 and 1985, 162 vehicles were converted to the Jaguar 2, which fires tube-launched, optically tracked, wire guided (TOW) missiles. Prior to 1995, the tank destroyers were a separate branch in the army but are now integrated into the mechanized infantry as the 6th company of a panzergrenadier battalion. The Jaguar platoon consist of five vehicles (two sections of two plus the platoon leader). The vehicles have excellent optics. The main differences between the Jaguar 1 and 2 are different optics and a different loading mechanism for the TOW missiles. The Jaguar 2 has 12 TOW missiles with a reload time of approximately five seconds. Reloading is done automatically, and the vehicle remains sealed to allow the crew to fight in an NBC environment.

SPECIFICATIONS

Type:	*anti-tank vehicle*
Crew:	*4*
Weight:	*25,500kg (56,100lb)*
Length:	*6.61m (21.68ft)*
Height:	*2.54m (8.33ft)*
Width:	*3.12m (10.23ft)*
Ground Clearance:	*0.45m (1.47ft)*
Vertical Obstacle:	*0.75m (2.46ft)*
Trench:	*2m (6.56ft)*
Gradient:	*58 percent*
Powerplant:	*Daimler-Benz MB 837 diesel*
Power Rating:	*500hp*
Speed – Maximum:	*70km/h (43.75mph)*
Cruising Range:	*400km (250 miles)*
Main Armament:	*1 x HOT ATGW launcher*
Secondary Armament:	*2 x 7.62mm*
Ammunition:	*12 x HOT, 3200 x 7.62mm*

LEOPARD 1

The Leopard 1 was first produced in 1963 and more than 6000 vehicles have since been exported to nine NATO countries: Belgium, Denmark, Germany, Greece, Italy, Canada, the Netherlands, Norway and Turkey, and also Australia. The main gun can fire while on the move through the use of an electronic, hydraulic gyroscopic gun stabilizer. This is known as a fully stabilized power traverse. In addition, the Leopard is fitted with two banks of smoke grenade dischargers on the turret to create local smoke screens. The Leopard can be sealed against nuclear contamination on the battlefield. It is a minimum-maintenance armoured fighting vehicle with visual lubricant level checks and minimum crew maintenance required: complete engine replacement is possible in 30 minutes under field conditions. With preparation, it is capable of deep-fording or submerged fording where river banks are prepared for exit and entry. A number of countries are upgrading their Leopard 1s. The Belgians, for example, are modernizing their old Leopard 1 BE (delivered from 1968) with the new 1A5. In 1978 Norway took delivery of 78 Leopard 1s, and the Norwegian vehicles underwent a modernization programme that replaced the hydraulic gun control system by an all-electric system, bringing them up to A5 standard.

SPECIFICATIONS

Type:	main battle tank
Crew:	4
Weight:	40,000kg (88,000lb)
Length (Gun Forward):	9.54kg (31.29ft)
Height:	2.61m (8.56ft)
Width:	3.37m (11.05ft)
Ground Clearance:	0.44m (1.44ft)
Vertical Obstacle:	1.15m (3.77ft)
Trench:	3m (9.84ft)
Gradient:	60 percent
Powerplant:	MTU MB 838 Ca M500
Power Rating:	830hp
Speed – Maximum:	65km/h (40.62mph)
Cruising Range:	600km (375 miles)
Main Armament:	1 x 105mm
Secondary Armament:	2 x 7.62mm
Ammunition:	60 x 105mm, 5500 x 7.62mm

LEOPARD 2

The successor to the Leopard 1, the Leopard 2, was first produced in 1979. A variety of upgrade programmes and options are available for the Leopard 2, including the vehicle Integrated Command and Information System (IFIS), a digital command and information system. The Leopard 2 has had technical improvements under Upgrading Level I and Level II programmes. For example, a new smoothbore gun, the 120mm L55 gun, has been developed by Rheinmetall GmbH to replace the shorter 120mm L44 smoothbore gun. It permits effective use of the new APFSDS-T round – DM53 (LKE II) – which has a longer rod penetrator. The German Army has decided not to purchase the DM43 APFSDS-T round, but rather wait and upgrade to the DM53. Combat support variants of the Leopard 2 include an armoured recovery vehicle. The Leopard 2A5/Leopard 2 (Improved) is a recent upgrade with spaced armour added to turret front, and increased armour on the hull and side skirts. Other improvements include improved stabilization, suspension, navigation, fire control and hatch design. The Leopard 2E is a derivative of the A5 version, developed under a programme of co-manufacture between Spain and Germany. There is no doubt that the Leopard 2 is one of the finest main battle tanks in the world.

SPECIFICATIONS

Type:	*main battle tank*
Crew:	*4*
Weight:	*62,000kg (136,400lb)*
Length (Gun Forward):	*9.97m (32.7ft)*
Height:	*3m (9.84ft)*
Width:	*3.74m (12.27ft)*
Ground Clearance:	*0.54m (1.77ft)*
Vertical Obstacle:	*1.1m (3.6ft)*
Trench:	*3m (9.84ft)*
Gradient:	*60 percent*
Powerplant:	*MTU MB 873 Ka 501*
Power Rating:	*1500hp*
Speed – Maximum:	*72km/h (45mph)*
Cruising Range:	*550km (344 miles)*
Main Armament:	*1 x 120mm*
Secondary Armament:	*2 x 7.62mm*
Ammunition:	*42 x 120mm, 4750 x 7.62mm*

LEOPARD 2A6

The Leopard 2A6 is equipped with the L55 gun, an auxiliary engine, improved mine protection and an air-conditioning system. The hull is in three sections: the driving compartment at the front, the fighting section in the centre and the engine at the rear of the vehicle. The driver's compartment is equipped with three observation periscopes, and the space to the left of the driver is provided for ammunition stowage. A camera with a 65-degree horizontal and vertical field of view positioned at the rear of the vehicle and a television monitor provide a reversing aid for the driver. An upgrade programme provides third-generation composite armour, and the additional reinforcement to the turret frontal and lateral armour with externally mounted add-on armour modules. In the event of weapon penetration through the armour, the spall liner reduces the number of fragments and narrows the fragment cone. The reinforcement provides protection against multiple strike, kinetic energy rounds and shaped charges. A new smoothbore gun, the 120mm L55, replaces the shorter 120mm L44 smoothbore gun on the Leopard 2. The extension of the barrel length from calibre length 44 to calibre length 55 results in a greater portion of the available energy in the barrel being converted into projectile velocity.

SPECIFICATIONS

Type:	main battle tank
Crew:	4
Weight:	62,000kg (136,400lb)
Length (Gun Forward):	9.97m (32.7ft)
Height:	3m (9.84ft)
Width:	3.74m (12.27ft)
Ground Clearance:	0.54m (1.77ft)
Vertical Obstacle:	1.1m (3.6ft)
Trench:	3m (9.84ft)
Gradient:	60 percent
Powerplant:	MTU MB 873 Ka 501
Power Rating:	1500hp
Speed – Maximum:	72km/h (45mph)
Cruising Range:	500km (312 miles)
Main Armament:	1 x 120mm
Secondary Armament:	2 x 7.62mm
Ammunition:	42 x 120mm, 4750 x 7.62mm

MARDER

First production vehicles of the Marder were delivered to the German Army in December 1970 and production continued until 1975. The chassis remained in production for the Roland SAM system until 1983. The driver sits left front with one infantryman behind him, with the engine compartment to his right. The troop compartment is in the rear with three infantrymen seated each side. Many vehicles have a Milan anti-tank missile above the commander's hatch on the right side of the turret. The Marder has a number of distinctive features: a well-sloped glacis plate, hull sides that slope inwards above the suspension, a power-operated ramp in the hull rear, a large turret with sloping front, sides and rear with an externally mounted 20mm cannon and smoke grenade launchers to left of the cannon; and the suspension each side has six large evenly spaced road wheels. There are a number of variants: Marder 1A1 with double-feed for a 20mm cannon, image intensification night sight with thermal pointer, new water can racks and flaps for periscopes; Marder 1A1A, upgraded in all areas except passive night vision equipment; Marder 1A2 with modified chassis and suspension; and Marder 1A3. All Marders are being upgraded to the 1A3 standard with improved armour and new roof hatch arrangement.

SPECIFICATIONS

Type:	*infantry combat vehicle*
Crew:	*3 + 6*
Weight:	*29,200kg (64,240lb)*
Length:	*6.79m (22.27ft)*
Height:	*2.98m (9.77ft)*
Width:	*3.24m (10.62ft)*
Ground Clearance:	*0.44m (1.44ft)*
Vertical Obstacle:	*1m (3.28ft)*
Trench:	*2.5m (8.2ft)*
Gradient:	*60 percent*
Powerplant:	*MTU MB 833 Ea 500 diesel*
Power Rating:	*600hp*
Speed – Maximum:	*65km/h (40.62mph)*
Cruising Range:	*520km (325 miles)*
Main Armament:	*1 x 20mm*
Secondary Armament:	*1 x 7.62mm, 1 x Milan*
Ammunition:	*1250 x 20mm, 5000 x 7.62mm*

MARS

MARS is the German version of the Multiple Launch Rocket System (MLRS). Entering service with the German Army in 1990, it is a high-mobility automatic system based on an M270 weapons platform. MLRS fires surface-to-surface rockets and the Army Tactical Missile System (ATACMS). Without leaving the cab, the crew of three (driver, gunner and section chief) can fire up to 12 MLRS rockets in less than 60 seconds. The MLRS launcher unit comprises an M270 Launcher loaded with 12 rockets, packaged in two six-rocket pods. The launcher, which is mounted on a stretched Bradley chassis, is a highly automated self-loading and self-aiming system. It contains a fire control computer that integrates the vehicle and rocket launching operations. The rockets can be fired individually or in ripples of 2 to 12. Accuracy is maintained in all firing modes because the computer re-aims the launcher between rounds. The MLRS can be transported to the area of operations by C-5 transport aircraft or by train. The basic MLRS tactical rocket warhead contains 644 M77 munitions, which are dispensed above the target in mid-air. The dual-purpose bomblets are armed during freefall and a simple drag ribbon orients the bomblets for impact. Each MLRS launcher can deliver almost 8000 munitions in less than a minute.

SPECIFICATIONS

Type:	*multiple launch rocket system*
Crew:	*3*
Weight:	*24,756kg (54,463lb)*
Length:	*7.16m (23.49ft)*
Height:	*2.57m (8.43ft)*
Width:	*2.97m (9.74ft)*
Ground Clearance:	*0.43m (1.41ft)*
Vertical Obstacle:	*0.61m (2ft)*
Trench:	*1.68m (5.51ft)*
Gradient:	*60 percent*
Powerplant:	*Detroit Diesel 6V53TIA*
Power Rating:	*500hp*
Speed – Maximum:	*64km/h (40mph)*
Cruising Range:	*480km (300 miles)*
Main Armament:	*12 rockets*
Secondary Armament:	*none*
Ammunition:	*none*

PZH 2000

The PzH 2000 (*Panzerhaubitze* 2000) is the 155mm self-propelled howitzer developed for the German Army. The first system was delivered in July 1998 and the total German Army requirement is expected to be around 450 units. The gun has a chromium-plated barrel and semi-automatic lifting breech block with integrated 32-round standard primer magazine. Gun parameters such as chamber temperature are monitored automatically. The PzH 2000 is equipped with a fully automatic shell loading system with an ammunition management system which can handle 60 rounds of 155mm ammunition in total. The shells are picked up from the back of the vehicle and automatically stowed in the 60-round magazine in the centre of the chassis. This gives an impressive rate of fire of 3 rounds in less than 10 seconds and loading of 60 shells by two operators within 12 minutes, including the collation of ammunition data. The PzH 2000 can use an automatic mode of operation, including the data radio link with an external command and control system. Using the automatic mode, target engagements can be carried out by a crew of two. Using the fire control data provided by the ballistics computer, the gun is automatically laid and relayed during the fire mission. Overall the PzH 2000 is an excellent mobile artillery platform.

SPECIFICATIONS

Type:	*self-propelled howitzer*
Crew:	*5*
Weight:	*55 000kg (121,000lb)*
Length (Gun Forward):	*11.67m (38.28ft)*
Height:	*3.06m (10ft)*
Width:	*3.58m (11.74ft)*
Ground Clearance:	*0.4m (1.31ft)*
Vertical Obstacle:	*1m (3.28ft)*
Trench:	*3m (9.84ft)*
Gradient:	*50 percent*
Powerplant:	*MTU MT 881 Ka 500 diesel*
Power Rating:	*1000hp*
Speed – Maximum:	*60km/h (37.5mph)*
Cruising Range:	*420km (262 miles)*
Main Armament:	*1 x 155mm*
Secondary Armament:	*1 x 7.62mm*
Ammunition:	*60 x 155mm, 1000 x 7.62mm*

WIESEL

The Wiesel 1 weapons carrier is based on a Porsche concept. Rheinmetall was the general contractor for the production and delivery of both Wiesel 1 versions to the German Airborne Brigades. Firepower, mobility and excellent means of survival characterize the Wiesel 1, as well as air transportability, flexibility and quick operational readiness. In addition, it has good all-round observation and target reconnaissance facilities and night combat ability. The TOW version has a crew of three men and, due to its anti-tank missile system, can hit targets accurately at ranges up to 3750m (12,203ft). The Wiesel 2 multi-purpose carrier was developed from the Wiesel 1, specifically with the requirement for more room and loading capacity due to the army's extended range of missions, i.e. for rapid-reaction and peacekeeping missions. The air transportability, light weight, high mobility and low silhouette of its predecessor were kept in all vehicle versions, but the length was increased by the size of one pair of road wheels. This resulted in twice as much space in the interior of the vehicle. Both systems complement each other perfectly in their ability to fulfil a broad spectrum of missions. They can be air transported as internal or external loads on helicopters and as internal loads on fixed-wing aircraft.

SPECIFICATIONS

Type:	airportable armoured vehicle
Crew:	3
Weight:	2800kg (6160lb)
Length:	3.31m (10.85kg)
Height:	1.89m (6.2ft)
Width:	1.82m (5.97ft)
Ground Clearance:	0.3m (0.98ft)
Vertical Obstacle:	0.4m (1.31ft)
Trench:	1.2m (3.93ft)
Gradient:	60 percent
Powerplant:	VW turbocharged diesel
Power Rating:	86hp
Speed – Maximum:	75km/h (46.87mph)
Cruising Range:	300km (187 miles)
Main Armament:	1 x TOW ATGW launcher
Secondary Armament:	none
Ammunition:	7 x TOW ATGW

AS90

The AS90 is a 155mm self-propelled howitzer which entered service with the British Army in 1992. The crew consists of the driver plus four or three operators in the cupola: a commander, a gun layer and an ammunition loader. An automated loading system enables the gun to fire with a burst rate of 3 rounds in under 10 seconds, an intense rate of 6 rounds per minute in three minutes and a sustained rate of 2 rounds per minute. The gun, which does not require stabilizing spades, is equipped with a recoil and hydrogas suspension system which allows the turret to traverse and fire through the full 360 degrees. A dynamic reference unit (DRU) and electronic compensation for tilt of the vehicle are used for accurate orientation of the weapon system. The range is 24.7km (15.43 miles) using conventional ammunition. Fitting a 52-calibre barrel instead of the standard 39-calibre extends the range beyond 40km (25 miles). An automated ammunition handling system is included in the current upgrade programme. The vehicle is of all-welded steel armour construction which is rated to withstand impact by 7.62mm and 14.5mm armour-piercing shells and 152mm shell fragments. A system for increased ballistic protection against top attack by current generation anti-tank missiles is being developed.

SPECIFICATIONS

Type:	*self-propelled howitzer*
Crew:	*4–5*
Weight:	*42,000kg (92,400lb)*
Length (Gun Forward):	*9.7m (31.82ft)*
Height:	*3m (9.84ft)*
Width:	*3.3m (10.82ft)*
Ground Clearance:	*0.4m (1.31ft)*
Vertical Obstacle:	*0.75m (2.46ft)*
Trench:	*2.8m (9.18ft)*
Gradient:	*60 percent*
Powerplant:	*Cummins V8 diesel*
Power Rating:	*660hp*
Speed – Maximum:	*55km/h (34.37mph)*
Cruising Range:	*350km (219 miles)*
Main Armament:	*1 x 155mm*
Secondary Armament:	*1 x 12.7mm*
Ammunition:	*48 x 155mm, 1000 x 12.7mm*

CHALLENGER 1

The Challenger main battle tank is a development of the Centurion/Chieftain line, modified to produce the Shir/Iran 2 originally planned for service with the Iranian Army. After the Iranian Revolution and the fall of the Shah, the Shir/Iran 2 project was taken over by the British Army and the end result was Challenger, later redesignated as Challenger 1. The main differences between Challenger 1 and its predecessor Chieftain are the engine, which produces 1200bhp at 2300rpm, far more powerful than the Chieftain engine, and the Chobham armour, which gives very high protection levels against anti-armour weapons. The Challenger 1 had been completely replaced by the Challenger 2 by the end of 2001, and some Challenger 1 hulls will be used for specialist vehicles. The Challenger has a 12-cylinder 1200hp Perkins diesel engine and a David Brown TN54 gearbox, with six forward and two reverse gears. The maximum speed by road is 59km/h (36.87mph) and 40km/h (25mph) cross country. As well as the main and secondary armaments, the tank is equipped with two five-shot smoke grenade dischargers mounted in the turret. The tank also has a full nuclear, biological and chemical (NBC) defence system, and the commander, gunner and driver have access to nright-vision equipment.

SPECIFICATIONS

Type:	*main battle tank*
Crew:	*4*
Weight:	*62,000kg (136,400lb)*
Length (Gun Forward):	*11.55mm (37.89ft)*
Height:	*2.49m (8.16ft)*
Width:	*3.51m (11.51ft)*
Ground Clearance:	*0.5m (1.64ft)*
Vertical Obstacle:	*0.9m (2.95ft)*
Trench:	*2.8m (9.18ft)*
Gradient:	*58 percent*
Powerplant:	*Perkins Condor CV12 diesel*
Power Rating:	*1200hp*
Speed – Maximum:	*59km/h (36.87mph)*
Cruising Range:	*450km (281 miles)*
Main Armament:	*1 x 120mm*
Secondary Armament:	*2 x 7.62mm*
Ammunition:	*64 x 120mm, 4000 x 7.62mm*

CHALLENGER 2

Challenger 2 is an advanced main battle tank which is in service with the British Army and with the Royal Army of Oman. Challenger 2 is equipped with an L30 120mm rifled tank gun, which is made from electro-slag refined steel (ESR) and is insulated with a thermal sleeve. It is fitted with a muzzle reference system and fume extraction. The turret is capable of 360-degree rotation and the weapon elevation range is from –10 to +20 degrees. There is capacity for 50 120mm projectiles, including armour-piercing, fin-stabilized, discarding sabot (APFSDS), high-explosive, squash head (HESH) or smoke rounds. The L30 gun can also fire the depleted uranium (DU) round with a stick charge propellant. With the DU round, the L30 is part of the Charm 1 gun, charge and projectile system. A Charm 3 system is under development in which the DU projectile has a higher length to diameter aspect ratio for increased penetration. Challenger 2E, the latest development model, has a new integrated weapon control and battlefield management system, which includes a gyrostabilized day/thermal sight for both commander and gunner. This allows hunter/killer operations with a common engagement sequence. An optional servo-controlled overhead weapons platform can also be fitted.

SPECIFICATIONS

Type:	*main battle tank*
Crew:	*4*
Weight:	*62,500kg (137,500lb)*
Length (Gun Forward):	*11.55mm (37.89ft)*
Height:	*2.49m (8.16ft)*
Width:	*3.51m (11.51ft)*
Ground Clearance:	*0.5m (1.64ft)*
Vertical Obstacle:	*0.9m (2.95ft)*
Trench:	*2.8m (9.18ft)*
Gradient:	*60 percent*
Powerplant:	*Perkins Condor CV12 diesel*
Power Rating:	*1200hp*
Speed – Maximum:	*59km/h (36.87mph)*
Cruising Range:	*450km (281 miles)*
Main Armament:	*1 x 120mm*
Secondary Armament:	*2 x 7.62mm*
Ammunition:	*50 x 120mm, 4000 x 7.62mm*

CHIEFTAIN

A round 900 Chieftains were built for the British Army with production being completed in the early 1970s. Although it is no longer in British frontline service, it is one of the great tanks of the twentieth century. There are a number of specialized variants of the tank which are still in service with the British Army. These include the Armoured Vehicle Royal Engineer (AVRE designated FV4203), Armoured Repair and Recovery Vehicle (ARRV), Armoured Recovery Vehicle (ARV designated FV4204) and Armoured Vehicle-Launched Bridge (AVLB designated FV4205), which carries the No. 8 or No. 9 Tank Bridge. Iran ordered 707 Chieftains in 1971 (Mk. 3/3(P) and Mk. 5/3(P)) with a number of armoured recovery vehicles and bridgelayers. Iran also took delivery of some 187 improved Chieftains, designated the FV4030/1. Oman bought a number of Chieftain Mk 15s (named *Qayd Al Ardh*) in the mid-1980s. The hull of the Chieftain is made of cast and rolled steel sections welded together. The Chieftain mounts a Royal Ordnance 120mm L11A5 rifled gun fitted with a Pilkington Optronics laser rangefinder. In the 1970s, British Army Chieftains were fitted with the thermal observation and gunnery sight (TOGS), a fully integrated improved fire control system and Stillbrew armour.

SPECIFICATIONS

Type:	*main battle tank*
Crew:	*4*
Weight:	*53,500kg (117,700lb)*
Length (Gun Forward):	*10.79m (35.4ft)*
Height:	*2.89m (9.48ft)*
Width:	*3.5m (11.48ft)*
Ground Clearance:	*0.5m (1.64ft)*
Vertical Obstacle:	*0.91m (2.98ft)*
Trench:	*3.14m (10.3ft)*
Gradient:	*60 percent*
Powerplant:	*Leyland L60 diesel*
Power Rating:	*750hp*
Speed – Maximum:	*48km/h (30mph)*
Cruising Range:	*500km (312 miles)*
Main Armament:	*1 x 120mm*
Secondary Armament:	*2 x 7.62mm, 1 x 12.7mm*
Ammunition:	*64 x 120mm, 6000 x 7.62mm*

FV 430

First introduced in 1962, the FV 430 series of armoured vehicles was developed to fulfil no less than 14 roles including command post armoured personnel carrier, ambulance, minelayer, recovery and repair vehicle, mortar carrier, radar or troop carrier. Totally NBC proof, it can carry up to 10 men and 2 crew and may be armed with a 7.62mm machine gun or turret-mounted L37 machine gun. The FV 432 will continue to provide the bulk of armoured transport for the British Army until replaced in the twenty-first century, probably with another vehicle with the same capacity (complete replacement with the Warrior infantry fighting vehicle would require an expanded fleet of vehicles as the Warrior's capacity is not as good). There are a number of variants of this vehicle: the FV 434 is a engineer vehicle with a crane capable of lifting an AFV engine pack. It includes a field repair kit and has a total carrying ability of 2703kg (5947lb). The crane has a radius of 2.25m (7.38ft) and can lift 3050kg (6710lb). The FV 439 is used by the Royal Signals as a mobile command post; it is a command type FV 432 fitted with extra radios and an erectable mast. The signals equipment is carried internally, with external mast ready for erection and extra stowage bins mounted externally on the vehicle.

SPECIFICATIONS

Type:	*armoured personnel carrier*
Crew:	*2 + 10*
Weight:	*15,280kg (33,616lb)*
Length:	*5.25m (17.22ft)*
Height:	*2.28m (7.48ft)*
Width:	*2.8m (9.18ft)*
Ground Clearance:	*0.5m (1.64ft)*
Vertical Obstacle:	*0.9m (2.95ft)*
Trench:	*2.05m (6.72ft)*
Gradient:	*60 percent*
Powerplant:	*Rolls-Royce K60 diesel*
Power Rating:	*240hp*
Speed – Maximum:	*52km/h (32.5mph)*
Cruising Range:	*580km (362 miles)*
Main Armament:	*1 x 7.62mm*
Secondary Armament:	*3 x smoke dischargers*
Ammunition:	*unknown*

SABRE

Sabre was brought into service in 1995 using a Scorpion chassis and the 30mm turret from the Combat Vehicle Reconnaissance (Tracked) (CVR(T)) Fox. It is almost identical to Scimitar but has a lower profile turret. Sabre is used by the British Army for close reconnaissance and is equipped with a Rarden Cannon and Hughes 7.62mm chain gun. In 1997 the Cummins Engine Company was chosen by the UK Ministry of Defence to supply diesel engines to re-power the British Army's fleet of Combat Vehicle Reconnaissance (Tracked) light armoured vehicles. The announcement, made on the opening day of the Royal Navy/British Army Equipment Exhibition (31 September), revealed that vehicles would be fitted with the Cummins B-series six-cylinder, 5.9-litre engine for Reliability Demonstration Trials. This was the first stage in a programme which will eventually see over 1300 CVR(T)s – which include Scimitar, Sabre, Samson, Sultan and Samaritan vehicles – re-engined. Cummins will develop the vehicle conversion kit for all variants. The army's family of CVR(T) vehicles, designed and produced by Alvis Vehicles, were the last British Army armoured fighting vehicles to be powered by a petrol engine. Around 140 Sabres are currently in service with the British Army.

SPECIFICATIONS

Type:	reconnaissance vehicle
Crew:	3
Weight:	8130kg (17,886lb)
Length (Gun Forward):	5.15m (16.89ft)
Height:	2.17m (7.11ft)
Width:	2.17m (7.11ft)
Ground Clearance:	0.35m (1.14ft)
Vertical Obstacle:	0.5m (1.64ft)
Trench:	2.05m (6.72ft)
Gradient:	60 percent
Powerplant:	Cummins BTA diesel
Power Rating:	190hp
Speed – Maximum:	80.5km/h (50.3mph)
Cruising Range:	644km (403 miles)
Main Armament:	1 x 30mm
Secondary Armament:	1 x 7.62mm
Ammunition:	40 x 30mm, 3000 x 7.62mm

SCIMITAR

The Scimitar is a variant of the Scorpion armoured reconnaissance vehicle which continues to serve in the British Army even though it is tactically obsolete. Some Scorpions have since been converted to the Scimitar configuration using 30mm Rarden turrets of the obsolete Fox armoured car. The Scimitar's 30mm Rarden gun is powerful enough to defeat enemy armoured reconnaissance vehicles and personnel carriers. Used by medium reconnaissance regiments and armoured infantry units for reconnaissance, the vehicle's weapon is mainly for self-defence. In the attack, a patrol of two Scimitars may provide fire support against a bridge or similar objective. In 2000, the Scimitar fleet underwent a Life Extension Programme (LEP). The major part of this upgrade was the replacement of the current Jaguar 4.2-litre petrol engine by a more fuel-efficient Cummins BTA 5.9-litre diesel engine developing 190hp, although there were some additional modifications. The LEP was carried out on the Scimitar and Sabre reconnaissance vehicles, Spartan armoured personnel carrier, Sultan command post vehicle, Samson recovery vehicle, Samaritan ambulance and the Striker anti-tank vehicle armed with Swingfire anti-tank missiles. Fast and with good viewing equipment, it is an ideal reconnaissance vehicle.

SPECIFICATIONS

Type:	reconnaissance vehicle
Crew:	3
Weight:	8070kg (17,754lb)
Length (Gun Forward):	5.15m (16.89ft)
Height:	2.1m (6.88ft)
Width:	2.2m (7.21ft)
Ground Clearance:	0.35m (1.14ft)
Vertical Obstacle:	0.5m (1.64ft)
Trench:	2.05m (6.72ft)
Gradient:	60 percent
Powerplant:	Cummins BTA diesel
Power Rating:	190hp
Speed – Maximum:	80km/h (50mph)
Cruising Range:	644km (403 miles)
Main Armament:	1 x 30mm
Secondary Armament:	1 x 7.62mm
Ammunition:	160 x 30mm, 3000 x 7.62mm

SCORPION

The veteran Scorpion reconnaissance vehicle was the first of the British Army's Combat Vehicle Reconnaissance (Tracked) (CVR(T)) family, and was originally developed to meet a British Army requirement for a tracked reconnaissance vehicle. The first production units were completed in 1972 armed with a 76mm gun and powered by a Jaguar 4.2-litre petrol engine. Since then Alvis has built more than 3000 Scorpion vehicles for the home and export market. The latest production model is powered by a more fuel-efficient diesel engine (Cummins) and is fitted with a Cockerill 90mm gun. A wide range of optional equipment is available including an NBC (nuclear, biological, chemical) protection system, image intensification or thermal night vision equipment, a powered turret, navigation system, air-conditioning system and flotation screens. The Scorpion light tank is in service with Belgium, Botswana, Brunei, Chile, Honduras, Indonesia, Iran, Ireland, Jordan, Malaysia, Nigeria, Oman, the Philippines, Spain, Tanzania, Thailand, Togo, United Arab Emirates and Great Britain. This includes both 76mm and 90mm versions and variants. The Scorpion was originally designed as a fully amphibious vehicle with preparation, but this ability was subsequently removed from British Army Scorpions.

SPECIFICATIONS

Type:	reconnaissance vehicle
Crew:	3
Weight:	8073kg (17,761lb)
Length (Gun Forward):	4.79m (15.71ft)
Height:	2.1m (6.88ft)
Width:	2.23m (7.54ft)
Ground Clearance:	0.35m (1.14ft)
Vertical Obstacle:	0.5m (1.64ft)
Trench:	2.05m (6.72ft)
Gradient:	60 percent
Powerplant:	Cummins BTA diesel
Power Rating:	190hp
Speed – Maximum:	80.5km/h (50.3mph)
Cruising Range:	644km (403 miles)
Main Armament:	1 x 76mm
Secondary Armament:	1 x 7.62mm
Ammunition:	40 x 76mm, 3000 x 7.62mm

SPARTAN

Spartan is a derivative of the CVR(T) vehicle (Combat Vehicle Reconnaissance (Tracked). The vehicles all shared the same engine, chassis and were made almost entirely of aluminum. The Spartan was the armoured personnel carrier (APC) of the series and was named thus due to the absence of turret and armament (other than the machine gun mounted for defensive purposes). The vehicle is small, and can only carry a maximum of four troops in its personnel compartment. Spartan is used by specialist troops which can include mortar fire control teams, or anti-aircraft teams equipped with Javelin missiles, or it can serve as an engineer command vehicle. Spartan is in use with a number of countries, and the design will serve well into this century. In 2000, for example, the Belgian Ministry of Defence delivered the first 50 of 100 ex-Belgian Army Spartan armoured personnel carrier variants to the Jordanian armed forces. The King Hussein Main Workshops in Zarqa have overhauled the first batch, which will shortly be issued to field units, including, it is believed, the élite Special Operations Command. The green and black camouflage pattern normally associated with operations in northwest Europe has been retained, as has the Spartan's original 190hp Jaguar 4.2-litre petrol engine.

SPECIFICATIONS

Type:	armoured personnel carrier
Crew:	3 + 4
Weight:	8172kg (17,978lb)
Length:	5.12m (16.79ft)
Height:	2.26m (7.41ft)
Width:	2.24m (7.34ft)
Ground Clearance:	0.35m (1.14ft)
Vertical Obstacle:	0.5m (1.64ft)
Trench:	2.05m (6.72ft)
Gradient:	60 percent
Powerplant:	Jaguar J60 No. 1 petrol
Power Rating:	190hp
Speed – Maximum:	80.5km/h (50.3mph)
Cruising Range:	483km (302 miles)
Main Armament:	1 x 7.62mm
Secondary Armament:	none
Ammunition:	3000 x 7.62mm

STARSTREAK

The Starstreak self-propelled high-velocity missile (SP HVM) system has been in service with the British Army since 1997. The missile consists of a two-stage solid propellant rocket motor, a separation system and three high-density darts. A pulse of power from the missile firing unit causes the first-stage motor to ignite, which accelerates the missile. Canted nozzles on the missile cause it to roll. The centrifugal force of the roll causes the fins to unfold for aerodynamic stability in flight. Once clear of the canister, the motor is jettisoned. The second-stage motor ignites and accelerates the missile to a velocity greater than Mach 4. A separation system at the front end of the motor contains three darts. The Starstreak SP HVM is mounted on a tracked Stormer vehicle. The system has eight rounds of Starstreak missiles ready to fire, with a further 12 missiles carried. The SP HVM is fitted with a roof-mounted Air Defence Alerting Device (ADAD), whose infrared scanner and processor provide target detection and prioritization and the system automatically slews the weapon sight onto the target. The use of ADAD requires that the vehicle be, briefly, stationary. A panoramic weapon sight is located at the front right of the vehicle. Thales Optronics has been awarded a contract to supply a new thermal sighting system for the British Army.

SPECIFICATIONS

Type:	self-propelled SAM
Crew:	3
Weight:	12,700kg (27,940lb)
Length:	5.27m (17.29ft)
Height:	3m (9.84ft)
Width:	2.76m (9ft)
Ground Clearance:	0.42m (1.37ft)
Vertical Obstacle:	0.6m (1.96ft)
Trench:	1.75m (5.74ft)
Gradient:	60 percent
Powerplant:	Perkins T6 diesel
Power Rating:	250hp
Speed – Maximum:	80km/h (50mph)
Cruising Range:	650km (406 miles)
Main Armament:	8 x Starstreak
Secondary Armament:	none
Ammunition:	12 x Starstreak

STORMER

Alvis Vehicles built the original Stormer armoured personnel carrier (APC), then known as the FV 433, in the 1970s using components of its Scorpion Combat Vehicle Reconnaissance (Tracked) range. Production of the Stormer began in 1982: three for the USA to evaluate and 25 for Malaysia to use in an armoured personnel carrier role. The British Army, which selected Stormer in 1986 to carry the Starstreak system, uses three versions of the vehicle: as a platform for the Starstreak system, a reconnaissance vehicle for Starstreak units, and a flatbed fitted with the Alliant Techsystems Volcano anti-tank mine-scattering system. Stormer can use various weapon systems, such as a two-person turret armed with a 25mm cannon. There is a wide range of optional equipment, including an NBC protection system, an amphibious kit, passive night-vision equipment, and an air-conditioning system. Indonesia is the newest Stormer customer and has received a number of variants, including the armoured personnel carrier, command post vehicle, ambulance, recovery, bridgelayer and logistics vehicle. Stormer is in use with a number of countries: Indonesia (50); Malaysia (25); Oman (4); and Great Britain (170 plus still on delivery). The only APC users are Indonesia and Malaysia.

SPECIFICATIONS

Type:	*armoured personnel carrier*
Crew:	*1 + 12*
Weight:	*12,700kg (27,940lb)*
Length:	*5.27m (17.29ft)*
Height:	*2.49m (8.16ft)*
Width:	*2.7m (9ft)*
Ground Clearance:	*0.42m (1.37ft)*
Vertical Obstacle:	*0.6m (1.96ft)*
Trench:	*1.75m (5.74ft)*
Gradient:	*60 percent*
Powerplant:	*Perkins T6/3544 diesel*
Power Rating:	*250hp*
Speed – Maximum:	*80km/h (50mph)*
Cruising Range:	*650km (406 miles)*
Main Armament:	*1 x 7.62mm*
Secondary Armament:	*none*
Ammunition:	*3000 x 7.62mm*

TRACKED RAPIER

Rapier has become one of the most successful low-altitude mobile surface-to-air missiles (SAMs) ever deployed. Highly mobile and capable of being mounted on a trailer or on a tracked vehicle, Rapier showed its worth in the 1982 Falklands War when it knocked out Argentine aircraft. The missile itself is intended to destroy low-altitude, fast-moving threats as well as helicopters. Tracked Rapier is an armoured mobile air defence system carrying eight missiles on a trainable launcher with the guidance systems installed in an armoured cab. The system was originally developed for the Shah of Iran's Army, but like the Shir main battle tank, eventually found a home with the British Army. Blindfire Rapier is a radar-equipped version of the Rapier SAM defence system used by the RAF Regiment and British Army for point air defence. The operator still retains the option of optical targeting if the radar fails to lock onto the target, but if the radar is selected the engagement sequence is automatic. The radar has a range of about 12km (7.5 miles). The system is in constant development and can be made ready to fire in less than 15 seconds. The Rapier system proved an effective anti-aircraft missile during the 1982 Falklands War, and will continue in service well into the twenty-first century.

SPECIFICATIONS

Type:	*self-propelled SAM*
Crew:	*3*
Weight:	*14,010kg (30,822lb)*
Length:	*6.4m (21ft)*
Height:	*2.78m (9.12ft)*
Width:	*2.8m (9.18ft)*
Ground Clearance:	*0.41m (1.34ft)*
Vertical Obstacle:	*0.6m (1.96ft)*
Trench:	*1.68m (5.51ft)*
Gradient:	*60 percent*
Powerplant:	*Detroit Diesel Model 6V-53*
Power Rating:	*210hp*
Speed – Maximum:	*48km/h (30mph)*
Cruising Range:	*300km (187 miles)*
Main Armament:	*8 x Rapier SAM*
Secondary Armament:	*none*
Ammunition:	*none*

WARRIOR

The Warrior infantry fighting vehicle carries a driver, commander, gunner and seven fully equipped soldiers, together with supplies and weapons for a 48-hour period in NBC conditions. The Warrior adapts to a range of roles with weapon fits ranging from machine guns to 90mm guns, mortars and missile systems. The aluminium armour construction provides protection against 14.5mm armour-piercing rounds, 155mm air burst shell fragments and 9kg (19.8lb) anti-tank mines. Enhanced protection against other threats can be provided with applique armour. The reconnaissance version is fitted with additional armoured protection against conventional and chemical attack: armour shielding covers the front, sides and the suspension of the vehicle. The reconnaissance vehicle is normally operated by a crew of three – the driver, commander and the gunner – and also has the capacity to accommodate a reconnaissance officer and additional surveillance kit. The vehicle is equipped with an electrically operated turret which can traverse through a full 360 degrees. The turret is fitted with a Boeing M242 chain gun on a stabilized mount which allows the gun to be used while the vehicle is in motion. The turret also has an M240 7.62mm machine gun and TOW missile launchers are mounted on each side.

SPECIFICATIONS

Type:	*infantry fighting vehicle*
Crew:	*3 + 7*
Weight:	*24,500kg (53,900lb)*
Length (Gun Forward):	*6.34m (20.8ft)*
Height:	*2.79m (9.15ft)*
Width:	*3.03m (9.94ft)*
Ground Clearance:	*0.49m (1.6ft)*
Vertical Obstacle:	*0.75m (2.46ft)*
Trench:	*2.5m (8.2ft)*
Gradient:	*60 percent*
Powerplant:	*Perkins CV8 TCA V-8 diesel*
Power Rating:	*550hp*
Speed – Maximum:	*75km/h (46.87mph)*
Cruising Range:	*660km (412 miles)*
Main Armament:	*1 x 30mm*
Secondary Armament:	*2 x TOW, 1 x 7.62mm*
Ammunition:	*250 x 30mm, 2000 x 7.62mm*

MERKAVA 2

The Merkava is the innovative design of Major-General Israel Tal, whose primary criterion was crew survivability. For example, the engine is in the front to provide protection for the crew and there is a special protective umbrella for the tank commander to enable protection from indirect fire with the hatches open. Special "spaced armour" is in use along with protected fuel and ammunition compartments. Rear ammunition stowage is combined with a rear entrance and exit. Since the rounds are stowed in containers that can be removed from the vehicle whenever necessary, this space can accommodate tank crewmen who have been forced to abandon their vehicles, or even infantrymen. Rear ammunition stowage allows replenishment much more easily than if rounds have to be replaced in a carousel in the hull centre. Tank crews have long admired Merkava's rear entrance and exit, recognizing that it allows them to mount and dismount unobserved by the enemy and provides an excellent escape route. The gunner's station is equipped with a thermal sight and a day sight with a television channel, which are stabilized in two axes. A laser rangefinder and target tracker are integrated into the gunner's sight. The commander's station is fitted with a sight which can be optically relayed to the gunner's sight.

SPECIFICATIONS

Type:	main battle tank
Crew:	4
Weight:	61,000kg (134,200lb)
Length (Gun Forward):	8.8m (28.87ft)
Height:	2.8m (9.18ft)
Width:	3.7m (12.13ft)
Ground Clearance:	0.47m (1.54ft)
Vertical Obstacle:	0.95m (3.11ft)
Trench:	3m (9.84ft)
Gradient:	70 percent
Powerplant:	1790-6A V-12 diesel
Power Rating:	900hp
Speed – Maximum:	46km/h (28.75mph)
Cruising Range:	400km (250 miles)
Main Armament:	1 x 105mm
Secondary Armament:	3 x 7.62mm, 1 x 60mm mortar
Ammunition:	62 x 105mm, 10,000 x 7.62mm

MERKAVA 3

The Merkava Mk 3 entered service with the Israeli Army at the beginning of 1990. The main features of the Mk 3 are a new suspension system, a 1200hp engine and new transmission, a higher-power main gun, and new armour protection. Ballistic protection is provided by special armour modules, which are attached to the tank by bolts. About 1000 Merkava Mk 2 and Mk 3 tanks are in service with the Israeli armed forces. The main gun is a 120mm smoothbore gun developed by Israeli Military Industries. The gun has a Vidco Industries thermal sleeve, which increases accuracy by preventing distortion through the effects of weather, heat and shock. The tank is fitted with the Amcoram LWS-2 laser warning system, with the threat warning display installed at the commander's station. The turret and hull are fitted with a modular armour system which can be changed in the field. The forward section of the turret is fitted with additional blocks of armour to provide extra protection against the latest generation of top attack anti-tank missiles. A skirt of chains with ball weights is installed on the lower half of the turret bustle. Incoming high-explosive, anti-tank (HEAT) projectiles detonate on impact with the chains instead of penetrating the turret ring. Sprung armour side skirts protect the wheels and tracks.

SPECIFICATIONS

Type:	*main battle tank*
Crew:	*4*
Weight:	*61,000kg (134,200lb)*
Length (Gun Forward):	*8.8m (28.87ft)*
Height:	*2.8m (9.18ft)*
Width:	*3.7m (12.13ft)*
Ground Clearance:	*0.47m (1.54ft)*
Vertical Obstacle:	*0.95m (3.11ft)*
Trench:	*3m (9.84ft)*
Gradient:	*70 percent*
Powerplant:	*AVDS-1790-9AR diesel*
Power Rating:	*1200hp*
Speed – Maximum:	*55km/h (34.37mph)*
Cruising Range:	*500km (312 miles)*
Main Armament:	*1 x 120mm*
Secondary Armament:	*3 x 7.62mm, 1 x 60mm mortar*
Ammunition:	*50 x 120mm, 10,000 x 7.62mm*

ARIETE

The Italian Ariete tank can engage stationary and moving targets in both day and night conditions, while the tank itself is stationary or on the move. The main gun is a 120mm smoothbore gun which is fitted with a thermal sleeve, a fume extraction system and a muzzle reference system. The gun is stabilized in two axes by hydraulic servoes and can fire all available types of ammunition including armour-piercing, fin-stabilized, discarding sabot (APFSDS) and high explosive, anti-tank (HEAT) rounds. The hull and turret are of all-welded steel construction with enhanced armour protection over the frontal arc. The crew is protected from nuclear, biological and chemical (NBC) warfare by an NBC protection system. The tank's fire control system includes a day/night stabilized commander's panoramic periscope sight, gunner's stabilized sight with thermal imager and laser rangefinder, and digital fire control computer. The digital fire control computer downloads data from the tank's meteorological and wind sensors, together with the tank attitude, barrel wear characteristics, ammunition and target data. The computer calculates the fire control algorithms and is used to control the gun, the sighting systems and the laser rangefinder. Ariete is currently in service with the Italian Army.

SPECIFICATIONS

Type:	*main battle tank*
Crew:	*4*
Weight:	*54,000kg (118,800lb)*
Length (Gun Forward):	*9.67m (31.72ft)*
Height:	*2.5m (8.2ft)*
Width:	*3.6m (11.81ft)*
Ground Clearance:	*0.48m (1.57ft)*
Vertical Obstacle:	*2.1m (6.88ft)*
Trench:	*3m (9.84ft)*
Gradient:	*60 percent*
Powerplant:	*Iveco V-12 MTCA diesel*
Power Rating:	*1300hp*
Speed – Maximum:	*65km/h (40.62mph)*
Cruising Range:	*550km (344 miles)*
Main Armament:	*1 x 120mm*
Secondary Armament:	*2 x 7.62mm*
Ammunition:	*40 x 120mm, 2500 x 7.62mm*

DARDO

The Dardo infantry fighting vehicle has a 25mm gun turret, but can also be fitted with a 30 or 60mm gun turret. It is intended to be the basic model of a family of vehicles to include a 120mm mortar carrier, command vehicle, ambulance and light tank with a 105mm gun turret. The Dardo's main weapon is the 25mm cannon which has a rate of fire of 600 rounds per minute (200 rounds of ammunition are carried in the turret ready to fire). Two 7.62mm machine guns are installed on the turret, one coaxial with the main gun. Two TOW anti-tank guided weapon launchers are installed, one on each side of the turret. The TOW missile, supplied by Raytheon Missile Systems Company, is a wire-guided, optically tracked missile with a maximum range of 3.75km (2.34 miles). The hull is of all-welded aluminium alloy with add-on steel armour plates for increased protection. The vehicle has a very low profile, with height of 2.64m (8.66ft) to the top of the turret, which decreases the radar and visual signature of the vehicle for enhanced survivability. Smoke grenade launchers, with four 80mm barrels per side, are installed on the front of the turret on either side of the main gun in the forward pointing direction. The crew compartment has five rifle ports, two on each side plus one in the rear ramp, for close defence.

SPECIFICATIONS

Type:	infantry fighting vehicle
Crew:	3 + 6
Weight:	23,000kg (50,600lb)
Length:	6.7m (21.98ft)
Height:	2.64m (8.66ft)
Width:	3m (9.84ft)
Ground Clearance:	0.4m (1.31ft)
Vertical Obstacle:	0.85m (2.78ft)
Trench:	2.5m (8.2ft)
Gradient:	60 percent
Powerplant:	Iveco 8260 V-6 diesel
Power Rating:	520hp
Speed – Maximum:	70km/h (43.75mph)
Cruising Range:	500km (312 miles)
Main Armament:	1 x 25mm
Secondary Armament:	2 x 7.62mm, 2 x TOW
Ammunition:	200 x 25mm

TYPE 74

The Type 74 is armed with the British-designed 105mm L7 type rifled tank gun manufactured under licence. New 105mm APFSDS and high-explosive, anti-tank, missile projectile (HEATMP) rounds were developed for the Type 74. The hydropneumatic suspension system, including the attitude controls, make the vehicle excellent for operation over rugged Japanese terrain. The vertical variability of the road wheel positions provides superior suspension capabilities, and leading-edge technology was integrated into the gun control and targeting devices, comprised of computerized laser rangefinders, fire control systems and gun stabilization systems. The choice of an electrically powered gun turret was validated when the 1973 Middle East war demonstrated that hydraulic-driven tank turrets were susceptible to fire. The Type 74 tank is equipped with floodlights with xenon lamps instead of tungsten lamps (the initial design of the floodlight filter measured 60cm [23.62in] in diameter and broke easily from the shock or air blast each time the gun was fired). Night-vision operating systems are based on models obtained through technical aid from the United States, and consist of the periscope-type hanging from the hatch above the driver's head. The Type 74 is equipped with the ruby laser type laser rangefinder.

SPECIFICATIONS

Type:	*main battle tank*
Crew:	*4*
Weight:	*38,000kg (83,600lb)*
Length (Gun Forward):	*9.42m (30.9ft)*
Height:	*2.48m (8.13ft)*
Width:	*3.18m (10.43ft)*
Ground Clearance:	*0.65m (2.13ft)*
Vertical Obstacle:	*1m (3.28ft)*
Trench:	*2.7m (8.85ft)*
Gradient:	*60 percent*
Powerplant:	*Mitsubishi 10ZF Type 22 diesel*
Power Rating:	*720hp*
Speed – Maximum:	*55km/h (46.87mph)*
Cruising Range:	*300km (187 miles)*
Main Armament:	*1 x 105mm*
Secondary Armament:	*1 x 7.62mm, 1 x 12.7mm*
Ammunition:	*55 x 105mm, 4500 x 7.62mm*

TYPE 90

Development of the Type 90 tank started in 1977, and it was accepted for service in 1990. The tank is equipped with the same Rheinmetall 120mm tank gun as the German Leopard 2. It carries a smoothbore barrel rather than a rifled barrel, and ammunition includes armour-piercing projectiles, anti-tank howitzer shells, and adhesive – high explosive plastic (HEP) – howitzer shells. With the exception of the turretless Swedish Stridsvagn (S-type) tank and various Russian models, the Type 90 tank is the first tank to achieve manpower savings by reducing the crew to three through the development of an ammunition autoloader. Innovative technology includes a laser and thermal-guided gun and turret controls. The automatic target tracking system using a thermal image display is controlled through the tank commander's targeting periscope attached to the top of the turret in an independently rotatable mode. Night-vision rangefinders are integrated into fire control systems and night-vision thermal imaging systems of a passive type use the infrared rays emitted from the opposing target to increase accuracy. These features enable the tank to achieve high-precision, mobile firing. Proprietary technology was used on the composite armour, including steel and ceramics with superior projectile-resistant qualities.

SPECIFICATIONS

Type:	*main battle tank*
Crew:	*3*
Weight:	*50,000kg (110,000lb)*
Length (Gun Forward):	*9.75m (31.98ft)*
Height:	*2.34m (7.67ft)*
Width:	*3.42m (11.22ft)*
Ground Clearance:	*0.45m (1.47ft)*
Vertical Obstacle:	*1m (3.28ft)*
Trench:	*2.7m (8.85ft)*
Gradient:	*60 percent*
Powerplant:	*Mitsubishi 10ZG diesel*
Power Rating:	*1500hp*
Speed – Maximum:	*70km/h (43.75mph)*
Cruising Range:	*400km (250 miles)*
Main Armament:	*1 x 120mm*
Secondary Armament:	*1 x 7.62mm, 1 x 12.7mm*
Ammunition:	*unknown*

2S1 M1974

Ever since the 2S1 was seen in public for the first time in 1974, it has been known under the provisional designation M1974. It also has been referred to as SP-74 and SAU-122. Although the 2S1 has been variously described as a gun, a gun-howitzer or a howitzer, the Soviet press called it a howitzer. The boat-like hull contains the engine compartment at the right front and the driver's compartment at the left front, with the driver's hatch to the left of the gun tube. The fighting compartment in the rear of the hull is topped by a low-silhouette, rotating turret. Atop the all-welded turret are the commander's cupola (with single hatch cover) on the left and the loader's hatch on the right. The gunner, also located in the left side of the turret, has no hatch. The commander and driver have infrared night-sighting equipment, but there is no infrared gunnery equipment. An interesting feature on the turret is the teardrop-shaped port cover on the left front near the gunner's position. The 2S1 has a direct fire sight besides its panoramic telescope and it is fitted with a collective NBC overpressure and filtration protective system. The 122mm howitzer mounted on the rounded front of the turret is derived from the towed howitzer D-30. The double-baffle muzzle brake is flush with the forward edge of the hull.

SPECIFICATIONS

Type:	self-propelled gun
Crew:	4
Weight:	15,700kg (34,540lb)
Length (Gun Forward):	7.26m (23.81ft)
Height:	2.72m (8.92ft)
Width:	2.85m (9.35ft)
Ground Clearance:	0.4m (1.31ft)
Vertical Obstacle:	0.7m (2.29ft)
Trench:	2.75m (9.02ft)
Gradient:	77 percent
Powerplant:	YaMZ-238 diesel
Power Rating:	300hp
Speed – Maximum:	60km/h (37.5mph)
Cruising Range:	500km (312 miles)
Main Armament:	1 x 122mm
Secondary Armament:	none
Ammunition:	40 x 122mm

2S3 M1973

The 2S3 was first introduced into the Soviet inventory in 1973 and has also been known under the provisional designation M1973. The 2S3 comprises a modified version of the 152mm towed howitzer D-20 and a chassis similar to the SA-4/Ganef launch vehicle. The thick gun tube extends beyond the front of the hull (the length of the double-baffle muzzle brake). It differs from the D-20 by the addition of a bore evacuator just behind the muzzle brake and, in travel position, it is supported by a brace attached just behind the bore evacuator. The 2S3 provides highly mobile, all-terrain fire support for motorized rifle and tank divisions, though is now a little old and outmoded. Its maximum range with a normal round is the same as that of the 152mm towed howitzer D-20 – 17.2km (10.75 miles) – and it also fires a long-range round, increasing its range to about 30km (18.75 miles). The 2S3M is an upgrade version of the 2S3. The 2S3M turret contains the 2A33 cannon, fire control equipment, ammunition storage space and work positions for commander, gunner and loader. The cannon extends beyond the vehicle front and has an electrical loader/rammer attached to the cradle. Ammunition is stored in the rear of the chassis and can be replenished through a hatch in the rear panel.

SPECIFICATIONS

Type:	*self-propelled gun*
Crew:	*4*
Weight:	*27,500kg (60,500lb)*
Length (Gun Forward):	*7.75m (25.42ft)*
Height:	*3.13m (10.26ft)*
Width:	*3.21m (10.53ft)*
Ground Clearance:	*0.45m (1.47ft)*
Vertical Obstacle:	*0.7m (2.29ft)*
Trench:	*3m (9.84ft)*
Gradient:	*60 percent*
Powerplant:	*V-59 V-12 water-cooled diesel*
Power Rating:	*520hp*
Speed – Maximum:	*60km/h (37.5mph)*
Cruising Range:	*450km (281 miles)*
Main Armament:	*1 x 152mm*
Secondary Armament:	*1 x 7.62mm*
Ammunition:	*46 x 152mm, 1500 x 7.62mm*

2S19 MSTA-S

The 152mm 2S19 MSTA-S self-propelled howitzer entered service with the Russian Army in 1989. While the Russian Army hoped to replace all of its 122mm and 152mm self-propelled artillery with this howitzer, financial constraints mean this replacement is unlikely. At least one 2S19-equipped regiment served in Chechnya as part of VIII Army Corps. MSTA-S comprises a turret mounted on a tracked armoured chassis based on elements of the T-72 and T-80 main battle tanks. The 2S19's gun crew can load the gun at any angle of elevation. Ammunition and gun loading, laying and re-targeting are highly automated, allowing a maximum firing rate of eight rounds per minute with onboard rounds and six or seven rounds per minute with rounds from the ground. The system provides automatic gun loading for projectiles and semi-automatic loading for charges. The design of the ammunition rack allows different types of projectiles to be stored in the same rack, and the automatic loading mechanism can select the type of ammunition and control the loading and the number of rounds. A battery can deliver projectiles on a target and move on to the next firing point before reaction firing. The howitzer's armour gives protection against armour-piercing bullets and projectiles and the 2S19 can also produce a smoke screen.

SPECIFICATIONS

Type:	self-propelled howitzer
Crew:	5
Weight:	42,000kg (92,400lb)
Length (Gun Forward):	11.91m (39.07ft)
Height:	2.98m (9.77ft)
Width:	3.58m (11.74ft)
Ground Clearance:	0.45m (1.47ft)
Vertical Obstacle:	0.5m (1.64ft)
Trench:	2.8m (9.18ft)
Gradient:	47 percent
Powerplant:	V84-A diesel
Power Rating:	840hp
Speed – Maximum:	60km/h (37.5mph)
Cruising Range:	500km (312 miles)
Main Armament:	1 x 152mm
Secondary Armament:	1 x 12.7mm
Ammunition:	50 x 152mm, 300 x 12.7mm

BMD-1

Although originally thought to be a light tank, the BMD is actually the airborne equivalent of the BMP infantry combat vehicle. However, except for the turret and main armament, it is an entirely new design and not a modified BMP. Excluding the obsolescent ASU-57, the BMD was the lightest tracked combat vehicle in the Soviet Red Army. The air-dropable BMD is considerably smaller and lighter than the BMP but has roughly the same capabilities. Its turret armour (maximum 25mm [0.98in]) is thicker than that of the BMP's, but its hull is thinner (maximum 15mm [0.59in]). An internal NBC filtration system provides protection for those inside the vehicle. Two squad members, including the squad leader, ride in the two hatch positions on each side of the driver, while the remaining three occupy the compartment between the turret and engine. The basic BMD was initially introduced around 1970 and within the following three or so years it underwent a variety of minor product-improvement modifications. The final design, designated BMD-1, is most readily identified by a dome-shaped NBC filter intake on the right-centre hull roof. The BMD-1 has retained the protection, mobility and firepower characteristics of the BMD and it can produce a smoke screen if need be.

SPECIFICATIONS

Type:	*airborne combat vehicle*
Crew:	*3 + 3*
Weight:	*13,300kg (26,600lb)*
Length:	*6.74m (22.11ft)*
Height:	*2.15m (7.05ft)*
Width:	*2.94m (9.64ft)*
Ground Clearance:	*0.45m (1.47ft)*
Vertical Obstacle:	*0.8m (2.62ft)*
Trench:	*1.6m (5.24ft)*
Gradient:	*60 percent*
Powerplant:	*diesel*
Power Rating:	*240hp*
Speed – Maximum:	*65km/h (40.62mph)*
Cruising Range:	*600km (375 miles)*
Main Armament:	*1 x 73mm*
Secondary Armament:	*2 x 7.62mm, 1 x AT-3 Sagger*
Ammunition:	*40 x 73mm, 2000 x 7.62mm*

BMD-3

The BMD-3 is more rugged than previous BMDs and can be airdropped with its complement of seven men inside the vehicle, enhancing the element of surprise associated with airborne operations. Previously, the crew of other vehicles would be dropped separately, requiring additional time to join up with their fighting vehicle. The all-welded construction of the BMD-3 provides the crew with protection from small-arms fire and shell splinters. The crew consists of commander, gunner, driver and four infantrymen, with the commander normally dismounting with the squad. Three additional infantrymen may be carried in an emergency in the rear. The two-man power-operated turret is armed with a 30mm 2A42 dual-feed cannon and a 7.62mm PKT machine gun mounted coaxially to the right. The roof-mounted ATGM launcher can fire either the AT-4 Spigot or AT-5 Spandrel. The bow-mounted AG-17 30mm automatic grenade launcher and 5.45mm RPKS machine gun are operated by the infantrymen seated in the front of the BMD-3. The automatic grenade launcher has 290 ready rounds and 261 in the rack. The ATGM launcher has 3 ready rounds (one on the launcher), and two stowed. Explosive reactive armour (ERA) is available for use on the BMD-3, but would be a hazard during troop dismounts.

SPECIFICATIONS

Type:	airborne combat vehicle
Crew:	3 + 4
Weight:	12,900kg (28,380lb)
Length:	6m (19.68ft)
Height:	2.25m (7.38ft)
Width:	3.14m (10.3ft)
Ground Clearance:	0.51m (1.67ft)
Vertical Obstacle:	0.8m (2.62ft)
Trench:	2.5m (8.2ft)
Gradient:	60 percent
Powerplant:	2V-06 water-cooled diesel
Power Rating:	450hp
Speed – Maximum:	70km/h (43.75mph)
Cruising Range:	600km (375 miles)
Main Armament:	1 x 30mm
Secondary Armament:	1 x 30mm, 1 x 7.62mm
	1 x 5.45mm, 1 x ATGM

BMP-1

A combination of effective anti-tank firepower, high mobility and adequate protection made the BMP a formidable addition to the inventory of Soviet motorized rifle units. Designed to suit the demands of high-speed offensive in a nuclear war, it carries a 73mm 2A20 gun with maximum rounds of 40 and maximum range of over 2134m (7000ft). The BMP has a three-man crew, including the vehicle commander, who becomes the squad leader when the infantry passengers dismount through the rear exit doors. However, vision blocks and firing ports in the sides and rear of the troop compartment allow the infantrymen to fire assault rifles and light machine guns from inside the vehicle on the move. The troops also carry the RPG-7 or RPG-16 anti-tank grenade launcher and the SA-7/Grail or SA-14 surface-to-air missile, either of which can be fired by a passenger standing in a rear hatch. When sealed in, crew and passengers have NBC protection in the pressurized and filtered hull, which allows them to operate regardless of the outside environment. The BMP is amphibious, propelled through water by its tracks rather than using the water-jet propulsion of the PT-76, and has the range and speed necessary to keep up with the fast-moving tanks it normally follows in offensive formations.

SPECIFICATIONS

Type:	infantry combat vehicle
Crew:	3 + 8
Weight:	13,500kg (44,291lb)
Length:	6.74m (22.11ft)
Height:	2.15m (7.05ft)
Width:	2.94m (9.64ft)
Ground Clearance:	0.39m (1.27ft)
Vertical Obstacle:	0.8m (2.62ft)
Trench:	2.2m (7.21ft)
Gradient:	60 percent
Powerplant:	UTD-20 water-cooled diesel
Power Rating:	300hp
Speed – Maximum:	65km/h (40.62mph)
Cruising Range:	600km (375 miles)
Main Armament:	1 x 73mm
Secondary Armament:	1 x 7.62mm, 1 x Sagger ATGW
Ammunition:	40 x 73mm, 2000 x 7.62mm

BMP-2

The BMP-2 (*Boyevaya Mashina Pyekhota* – Infantry Fighting Vehicle) infantry combat vehicle, fielded in the early 1980s, is an improved version of the BMP-1 incorporating major armament changes. The new two-man turret mounts a 30mm automatic gun with a long thin tube and double-baffle muzzle brake that can be used against aircraft and helicopters. The ATGM launcher on top of the turret can employ either AT-4 Spigot or AT-5 Spandrel missiles, though the AT-5 Spandrel canister is normally mounted. Given the enlarged turret, there are two roof hatches in the rear fighting compartment, rather than the four of the BMP-1, and the BMP-2 accommodates one less passenger. Each side of the troop compartment has three firing ports with associated roof-mounted periscopes. Other options are spall liners, air conditioning and a more powerful engine. An AG-17 30mm automatic grenade launcher modification is offered for the BMP-2, and there is also a drop-in one-man turret, called *Kliver*, with a stabilized 2A72 30mm gun, a four Kornet ATGM launcher, thermal sights, a coaxial 7.62mm machine gun and improved fire control system. The ATGM load consists of one ready on the launcher and four stowed. Thermal sights are available, and the Russian SANOET-1 thermal gunner's sight is available.

SPECIFICATIONS

Type:	*infantry combat vehicle*
Crew:	*3 + 7*
Weight:	*14,300kg (31,460lb)*
Length:	*6.72m (22.04ft)*
Height:	*2.45m (8.03ft)*
Width:	*3.15m (10.33ft)*
Ground Clearance:	*0.42m (1.37ft)*
Vertical Obstacle:	*0.7m (2.29ft)*
Trench:	*2.5m (8.2ft)*
Gradient:	*60 percent*
Powerplant:	*Model UTD-20 6-cylinder diesel*
Power Rating:	*300hp*
Speed – Maximum:	*65km/h (40.62mph)*
Cruising Range:	*600km (375 miles)*
Main Armament:	*1 x 30mm*
Secondary Armament:	*1 x 7.62mm, 1 x Spandrel ATGM*
Ammunition:	*500 x 30mm, 2000 x 7.62mm*

BMP-3

The BMP-3 infantry fighting vehicle represents a totally different design concept from the BMP-1 and 2 vehicles, because it is essentially a light tank that can hold a squad of infantry. It has a 100mm main gun that fires high-explosive rounds to demolish buildings, can fire long-range ATGMs through its barrel, and a 30mm autocannon and a medium machine gun as a single unit in the turret. This innovative BMP-3 armament suite has been subjected to criticism in the Russian military, which has focused on deficiencies in the barrel-fired ATGM. The hull of the BMP-3 resembles the BMD airborne infantry fighting vehicle in appearance, with a new turret in the centre of the vehicle. The troop compartment at the rear of the hull is accessed via a pair of doors in the hull rear. The BMP-3 is fully amphibious, propelled in water by two water-jets mounted at the rear of the hull. A drop-in one-man turret called *Kliver* is available, with a stabilized 2A72 30mm gun, a four Kornet ATGM launcher, thermal sights and improved fire control system. Stowed rounds and ATGMs can be passed from the passenger compartment to the gunner for hand loading, including ATGMs. The so-called "HEF"— high-explosive shrapnel — round can be employed in indirect fire mode with air burst up to a range of 7km (4.37 miles).

SPECIFICATIONS

Type:	*infantry fighting vehicle*
Crew:	*3 + 7*
Weight:	*18,700kg (41,140lb)*
Length (Gun Forward):	*7.2m (23.62ft)*
Height:	*2.45m (8.03ft)*
Width:	*3.14m (10.3ft)*
Ground Clearance:	*0.51m (1.67ft)*
Vertical Obstacle:	*0.8m (2.62ft)*
Trench:	*2.5m (8.2ft)*
Gradient:	*60 percent*
Powerplant:	*UTD-29 diesel*
Power Rating:	*500hp*
Speed – Maximum:	*70km/h (43.75mph)*
Cruising Range:	*600km (375 miles)*
Main Armament:	*1 x 100mm*
Secondary Armament:	*1 x 30mm, 3 x 7.62mm*
Ammunition:	*40 x 100mm, 500 x 30mm*

BTR-50P

The BTR-50P is based on the chassis of the PT-76 light amphibious tank with an open-topped troop compartment in the centre. The 20 infantrymen sit on bench seats which run across the full width of the vehicle and enter and leave by climbing over the side of the hull. Armament consists of a pintle-mounted 7.62mm machine gun. The BTR-50P is fully amphibious and propelled in the water by two water-jets at the rear of the hull. It is no longer in production and is being replaced by newer BTRs and BMPs in the Russian Army. However, given the parlous state of Russian finances, this process may take some time. Armoured personnel carriers of the BTR-50P series were issued to the motorized rifle regiment of tank divisions in the Soviet and East German Armies and have also been exported to the Middle East. The BTR-50P, which was first shown in public in November 1957, has undergone a number of modifications. The original BTR-50P had an open-topped fighting compartment, and at first carried no armament. There is now provision, however, for transporting 57mm, 76mm or 85mm guns in the fighting compartment. The guns are loaded onto the vehicle using folding ramps attached to the rear deck. The guns can be fired from the vehicle on land or in the water.

SPECIFICATIONS

Type:	armoured personnel carrier
Crew:	2 + 20
Weight:	14,200kg (31,240lb)
Length:	7.08m (23.22ft)
Height:	1.97m (6.46ft)
Width:	3.14m (10.3ft)
Ground Clearance:	0.37m (1.21ft)
Vertical Obstacle:	1.1m (3.6ft)
Trench:	2.8m (9.18ft)
Gradient:	60 percent
Powerplant:	Model V-6 water-cooled diesel
Power Rating:	240hp
Speed – Maximum:	44km/h (27.5mph)
Cruising Range:	400km (250 miles)
Main Armament:	1 x 7.62mm
Secondary Armament:	none
Ammunition:	1250 x 7.62mm

MT-LB

The MT-LB is an amphibious armoured tracked vehicle with a low-silhouette, box-like hull made of welded steel plates and a small turret on the right front, mounting a single 7.62mm machine gun. Its design is based on the MT-L light transport vehicle and prime mover. The MT-L, which is unarmoured and turretless, was first developed for geological research in the far north of the old Soviet Union. There are four firing ports, one on each side of the vehicle and one in each of the two rear exit doors. Two additional, forward-opening troop exit hatches are located on the flat hull roof. The flat-track suspension consists of six road wheels with no return rollers. The MT-LB can employ an extra-wide track with an "aggressive" grouser to make over snow and swamp operations easier. The MT-LB is a multi-purpose vehicle. For example, when used as a command vehicle it can carry 10 personnel besides its two-man crew (driver and commander-gunner). It is also used as a prime mover for various types of artillery. In this case it can also carry the artillery crew (six to 10 personnel). It is frequently used as prime mover for the T-12 artillery piece. The T-12 is a 100mm smoothbore anti-tank gun mounted on a two-wheeled, split-trail carriage, with a single caster wheel near the trail ends.

SPECIFICATIONS

Type:	multi-purpose tracked vehicle
Crew:	2 + 10
Weight:	11,900kg (26,180lb)
Length:	6.45m (21.16ft)
Height:	1.86m (6.1ft)
Width:	2.86m (9.38ft)
Ground Clearance:	0.4m (1.31ft)
Vertical Obstacle:	0.61m (2ft)
Trench:	2.41m (7.9ft)
Gradient:	60 percent
Powerplant:	YaMZ 238 V, V-8 diesel
Power Rating:	240hp
Speed – Maximum:	61.5km/h (38.43mph)
Cruising Range:	500km (312 miles)
Main Armament:	1 x 7.62mm
Secondary Armament:	none
Ammunition:	2500 x 7.62mm

PT-76

The PT-76 is one of several light amphibious tanks developed and used by the Russian Army. The vehicle entered service in 1954 and is amphibious without additional preparation. Although it is lightly armoured and undergunned for a modern tank, its inherent amphibious capability outweighs these limitations. It carries a 76mm main gun with a maximum effective range of approximately 1500m (4929ft). Operated by a three-man crew, the PT-76 is often used to transport troops. It has a flat, boat-like hull and the suspension has six road wheels and no return rollers. A dish-type turret is mounted over the second, third and fourth road wheels, with a double hatch for commander and loader. The driver's hatch is located beneath the main gun, at the top of the sloping glacis plate. Although it has been replaced in first-line units by the BMP-1 and BMP M1976 vehicles, it may still be found in the reconnaissance companies and battalions of some motorized rifle and tank regiments and divisions, as well as in naval infantry units. Aside from its reconnaissance role, it is also used for crossing water obstacles in the first wave of an attack and for artillery support during the establishment of a beachhead. It is in use in at least 21 countries, including those of the former Warsaw Pact.

SPECIFICATIONS

Type:	*amphibious tank*
Crew:	*3*
Weight:	*14,000kg (30,800lb)*
Length (Gun Forward):	*6.91m (22.67ft)*
Height:	*2.25m (7.38ft)*
Width:	*3.14m (10.3ft)*
Ground Clearance:	*0.51m (1.67ft)*
Vertical Obstacle:	*1.1m (3.6ft)*
Trench:	*2.8m (9.18ft)*
Gradient:	*70 percent*
Powerplant:	*Model V-6B diesel*
Power Rating:	*240hp*
Speed – Maximum:	*44km/h (27.5mph)*
Cruising Range:	*260km (162 miles)*
Main Armament:	*1 x 76mm*
Secondary Armament:	*1 x 7.62mm*
Ammunition:	*40 x 76mm, 1000 x 7.62mm*

SA-13 GOPHER

The Russian SA-13 Gopher mobile surface-to-air missiles (SAM) system is based on an MT-LB tracked vehicle. It provides short-range, low-altitude air defence and is replacing the less capable SA-9 system. The SA-13 missile is infrared-guided; the system is equipped with a range-only radar which enables the crew to ensure that the target is within the missile's effective range before firing. Introduced in 1980, it saw combat in Chad and Angola (in both theatres launchers were captured by pro-Western forces and were subsequently supplied to Western intelligence services for analysis). It was also used by Iraq in the Gulf War in 1991. Each vehicle carries four missiles with eight reloads in the cargo compartment. The SA-13 (Strela-10) missile uses an uncooled lead sulphide near-infrared homing type seeker with countermeasures capabilities against infrared decoys. Additionally, it operates in two frequencies to further counter infrared countermeasures. The system can be used against diverse and extremely low-altitude targets as well as in adverse weather. Two variants of the vehicle have been identified. Appraisal of both does not show any significant structural differences, but one carries four HAT BOX passive radars. The launcher vehicle is also capable of firing SA-9 missiles, if required.

SPECIFICATIONS

Type:	self-propelled SAM
Crew:	3
Weight:	12,300kg (27,060lb)
Length:	6.6m (21.65ft)
Height:	3.8m (12.46ft)
Width:	2.85m (9.35ft)
Ground Clearance:	0.4m (1.31ft)
Vertical Obstacle:	0.7m (2.29ft)
Trench:	2.7m (8.85ft)
Gradient:	60 percent
Powerplant:	YaMZ-238V diesel
Power Rating:	240hp
Speed – Maximum:	61.5km/h (38.43mph)
Cruising Range:	500km (312 miles)
Main Armament:	4 x SA-13 SAM
Secondary Armament:	none
Ammunition:	8 x SA-13 SAM

T-64

The T-64, introduced in the late 1960s, was the first of a sophisticated new family of Soviet main battle tanks developed as successors to the T-54/55/62 family. The hull and turret are of cast and welded steel armour incorporating both conventional steel armour and ceramic inserts, which provide superior protection against HEAT rounds. Besides having greatly increased frontal armour protection due to the use of improved layered armour, the T-64 can also attach track protection plates or full-length skirts. Low-flash fuel storage also offers protection to the sides. A front-mounted shovel enables the tank to dig itself in within a few minutes and also increases the armour protection of the lower hull front when it is folded upwards. The 125mm smoothbore main gun fires a hyper-velocity, armour-piercing, fin-stabilized, discarding sabot round believed to have a muzzle velocity of over 1750 metres (5740 feet) per second and an effective range of at least 2000m (6562ft). An automatic loader allows the crew to be reduced to three (commander, gunner and driver), and an automatic spent-cartridge ejection system is employed. The commander is capable of operating all weapons in the tank from his position. The T-64 has an improved, integrated fire control system. It has an onboard computer, and some variants may have a laser rangefinder.

SPECIFICATIONS

Type:	*main battle tank*
Crew:	*3*
Weight:	*39,500kg (86,900lb)*
Length (Gun Forward):	*9.2m (30.18ft)*
Height:	*2.2m (7.21ft)*
Width:	*3.4m (11.15fft)*
Ground Clearance:	*0.37m (1.21ft)*
Vertical Obstacle:	*0.8m (2.62ft)*
Trench:	*2.28m (7.48ft)*
Gradient:	*60 percent*
Powerplant:	*Model 5DTF 5-cylinder diesel*
Power Rating:	*750hp*
Speed – Maximum:	*75km/h (46.87mph)*
Cruising Range:	*400km (250 miles)*
Main Armament:	*1 x 125 mm*
Secondary Armament:	*1 x 7.62mm, 1 x 12.7mm*
Ammunition:	*36 x 125mm, 1250 x 7.62mm*

T-72

The T-72, introduced in the early 1970s, is not a further development of the T-64 but rather a parallel design chosen as a high-production tank complementing the T-64 fleet. The T-72 has greater mobility than the T-62, and its V-12 diesel engine has an output of 780hp. This engine appears to be remarkably smoke-free and smooth-running, having eliminated the excessive vibration which was said to cause high crew fatigue in the T-62. The T-72 has better armour protection than the T-62, due to the use of layered armour. The advanced passive armour package of the T-72M and T-72M1 can sustain direct hits from the 105mm gun-equipped M1 Abrams at up to a range of 2000m (6562ft) and survive. The later T-72Ms and T-72M1s are equipped with laser rangefinders ensuring high hit probabilities at ranges of 2000m (6562ft) and below. The 125mm gun common to all the T-72 models is capable of penetrating the M1 Abrams armour at a range of up to 1000m (3281ft). The more recent BK-27 high-explosive, anti-tank (HEAT) round offers a triple-shaped charge warhead and increased penetration against conventional armours and explosive reactive armour (ERA). The BK-29 round, with a hard penetrator in the nose, is designed for use against reactive armour, and also has fragmentation qualities.

SPECIFICATIONS

Type:	*main battle tank*
Crew:	*3*
Weight:	*44,500kg (97,900lb)*
Length (Gun Forward):	*9.53m (31.26ft)*
Height:	*2.22m (7.28ft)*
Width:	*3.59m (11.77ft)*
Ground Clearance:	*0.47m (1.54ft)*
Vertical Obstacle:	*0.85m (2.78ft)*
Trench:	*2.8m (9.18ft)*
Gradient:	*60 percent*
Powerplant:	*V-46 V-12 diesel*
Power Rating:	*780hp*
Speed – Maximum:	*60km/h (37.5mph)*
Cruising Range:	*500km (312 miles)*
Main Armament:	*1 x 125mm*
Secondary Armament:	*1 x 7.62mm, 1 x 12.7mm*
Ammunition:	*45 x 125mm, 2000 x 7.62mm*

T-80

The T-80 was the first Soviet operational tank to be powered by a gas turbine engine, with a GTD-1000 gas turbine engine developing 1100hp. The T-80 was also the first production Soviet tank to incorporate a laser rangefinder and ballistic computer system. The original night sight is the II Buran-PA. The 12.7mm machine gun has both remote electronically operated sight PZU-5 and gun-mounted K10-T reflex sight. The day sight can be used at night for launching anti-tank guided missiles (ATGMs) if the target is illuminated. A variety of thermal sights is available, including the Russian Agava-2, French ALIS and Namut sight from Peleng. When fitted with explosive reactive armour (ERA) the T-80 is virtually immune over its frontal arc to penetration from all current NATO ATGMs which rely on a high-explosive, anti-tank (HEAT) warhead to penetrate armour. On the turret of the T-80, the panels are joined to form a shallow chevron pointing. Explosive reactive armour is also fitted to the forward part of the turret roof to provide protection against top-attack weapons. However, the explosive reactive armour does not provide any added protection against armour-piercing, discarding sabot (APDS) or armour-piercing, fin-stabilized, discarding sabot (APFSDS) attack.

SPECIFICATIONS

Type:	main battle tank
Crew:	3
Weight:	46,000kg (101,200lb)
Length (Gun Forward):	9.66m (31.69ft)
Height:	2.2m (7.21ft)
Width:	3.6m (11.81ft)
Ground Clearance:	0.38m (1.24ft)
Vertical Obstacle:	1m (3.28ft)
Trench:	2.85m (9.35ft)
Gradient:	60 percent
Powerplant:	GTD-1000 gas turbine
Power Rating:	1100hp
Speed – Maximum:	70km/h (43.75mph)
Cruising Range:	600km (375 miles)
Main Armament:	1 x 125mm gun/missile launcher
Secondary Armament:	1 x 7.62mm, 1 x 12.7mm
Ammunition:	36 x 125mm, 1250 x 7.62mm

T-84

The T-84 is a Ukrainian upgrade of the T-80UD with a welded turret, a French thermal sight, a more powerful engine, optional use of an Arena active protection system (APS) and SHTORA-1 active infrared ATGM jammer system. The tank fire control system is the 1A42 which includes the 1V517 ballistic computer, two-axis electrohydraulic weapon stabilizer, rangefinder sight stabilized in two axes as well as a GPK-59 hydro-semicompass azimuth indicator and an azimuth indicator for the turret rotation. This system permits firing on the move. The gunner has the 1G46 day sight and also an infrared sight. The T-80U's gas turbine engine is the GTD-1250 which produces 1250 hp. The GTD-1250 is a three-shaft engine with two cascades of turbo-compression. There is also an independent GTA-18 auxiliary power unit for use when the tank is stationary. The tank has a planetary power transmission with hydraulic servo-system for increased mobility. The track and suspension system is fitted with track and rubber-tyred road wheels, torsion bar suspension with hydraulic telescopic double-acting shock absorbers. The main gun can fire a range of ammunition, including AP (armour-piercing), APDS (armour-piercing, discarding sabot), HEAT (high-explosive, anti-tank) and HE-FRAG (high-explosive fragmentation).

SPECIFICATIONS

Type:	*main battle tank*
Crew:	*3*
Weight:	*46,000kg (101,200lb)*
Length (Gun Forward):	*9.66m (31.69ft)*
Height:	*2.2m (7.21ft)*
Width:	*3.6m (11.81ft)*
Ground Clearance:	*0.38m (1.24ft)*
Vertical Obstacle:	*1m (3.28ft)*
Trench:	*2.85m (9.35ft)*
Gradient:	*60 percent*
Powerplant:	*GTD-1250 gas turbine*
Power Rating:	*1250hp*
Speed – Maximum:	*70km/h (43.75mph)*
Cruising Range:	*600km (375 miles)*
Main Armament:	*1 x 125mm gun/missile launcher*
Secondary Armament:	*1 x 7.62mm, 1 x 12.7mm*
Ammunition:	*36 x 125mm, 1250 x 7.62mm*

T-90

The T-90 is the latest development in the T-series of Russian tanks and represents an increase in firepower, mobility and protection. Armament includes one 125mm 2A46M smoothbore gun, stabilized in two axes and fitted with a thermal sleeve. The gun tube can be replaced without dismantling inside the turret, and the gun can fire a variety of ammunition including APDS (armour-piercing, discarding sabot), HEAT (high-explosive, anti-tank), HE-FRAG (high-explosive fragmentation) as well as shrapnel projectiles with time fuses. The T-90S gun can also fire the AT-11 Sniper anti-tank guided missile (ATGM) system. The tank is protected by both conventional armour plating and explosive reactive armour (ERA) and is fitted with the Shtora-1 defensive aids suite. This system includes infrared jammer, laser warning system with four laser warning receivers, grenade discharging system which produces an aerosol screen, and a computerized control system. It is also fitted with NBC (nuclear, biological and chemical) protection equipment. The T-90S has the 1A4GT integrated fire control system, which is automatic but with manual override for the commander. The IFCS contains the gunner's 1A43 day fire control system, gunner's TO1-KO1 thermal imaging sight and commander's PNK-S sight.

SPECIFICATIONS

Type:	*main battle tank*
Crew:	*3*
Weight:	*46,500kg (102,300lb)*
Length (Gun Forward):	*9.53m (31.26ft)*
Height:	*2.2m (7.21ft)*
Width:	*3.78m (12.4ft)*
Ground Clearance:	*0.47m (1.54ft)*
Vertical Obstacle:	*0.8m (2.62ft)*
Trench:	*2.8m (9.18ft)*
Gradient:	*60 percent*
Powerplant:	*V-84MS diesel*
Power Rating:	*840hp*
Speed – Maximum:	*unknown*
Cruising Range:	*500km (312 miles)*
Main Armament:	*1 x 125mm*
Secondary Armament:	*1 x 7.62mm, 1 x 12.7mm*
Ammunition:	*43 x 125mm, 2000 x 7.62mm*

TUNGUSKA

Tunguska-M1 is a gun/missile system for low-level air defence. The Tunguska-M1 vehicle carries eight 9M311-M1 surface-to-air missiles. The missile (NATO designation SA-19 Grison) has semi-automatic radar command to line-of-sight guidance, and weighs 40kg (88lb) with a 9kg (19.8lb) warhead. Two twin-barrel 30mm anti-aircraft guns are also mounted on the vehicle. These guns have a maximum firing rate of 5000 rounds per minute and a range of 3000m (9842ft) against air targets. This extends to 4000m (13,123ft) against ground targets. The system has a target acquisition radar and target tracking radar, optical sight, digital computing system, tilt angle measuring system and navigation equipment. Radar detection range is 18km (11.25 miles) and tracking range is 16 km (10 miles). The Tunguska-M1 system is mounted on a tracked vehicle with a multi-fuel engine. It has hydromechanical transmission, hydropneumatic suspension which allows for changing road clearance and hydraulic track-tensioning. The armoured turret has both laying and stabilization drives and power supply. Air-conditioning, heating and filtration systems are also fitted. A Tunguska-M1 battery comprises up to six vehicles and includes a transloader as well as maintenance and training facilities.

SPECIFICATIONS

Type:	*self-propelled SAM*
Crew:	*4*
Weight:	*34,000kg (74,800lb)*
Length:	*7.93m (26.01ft)*
Height:	*4.02m (13.18ft)*
Width:	*3.24m (10.62ft)*
Ground Clearance:	*unknown*
Vertical Obstacle:	*1m (3.28ft)*
Trench:	*2m (6.56ft)*
Gradient:	*60 percent*
Powerplant:	*V-12 turbocharged diesel*
Power Rating:	*500hp*
Speed – Maximum:	*65km/h (40.62mph)*
Cruising Range:	*500km (312 miles)*
Main Armament:	*4 x 30mm, 8 x SA-19 SAM*
Secondary Armament:	*none*
Ammunition:	*1904 x 30mm, 8 x SA-19 SAM*

ZSU-23-4 SHILKA

The ZSU-23-4 is a fully integrated, self-propelled anti-aircraft system with four liquid-cooled 23mm automatic cannons mounted on the front of a large, flat, armoured turret. The chassis has many components borrowed from other Soviet armoured vehicles, and the suspension system resembles that of the PT-76 and ASU-85 (six road wheels and no track support rollers). The driver sits in the left front of the hull, and the rest of the crew (commander, gunner and radar operator) is located in the turret. The Gun Dish fire control radar mounted on the rear of the turret can be folded down during travel. The ZSU-23-4 has the capability to both acquire and track low-flying aircraft targets, with an effective anti-aircraft range of 2500m (8202ft). It also is capable of firing on the move because of its integrated radar/gun stabilization system. The high frequency operation of the radar emits a very narrow beam that provides for excellent aircraft tracking while being difficult to detect or evade. However, such a frequency also dictates a limited range, which can be compensated for by linking the system to other long-range acquisition radars in the area. The ZSU-23-4 also can be used against lightly armoured vehicles. The four guns have a cyclic rate of fire of 800–1000 rounds per minute each.

SPECIFICATIONS

Type:	*self-propelled anti-aircraft gun*
Crew:	*4*
Weight:	*20,500kg (45,100lb)*
Length:	*6.54m (21.45ft)*
Height:	*3.8m (12.46ft)*
Width:	*2.95m (9.67ft)*
Ground Clearance:	*0.4m (1.31ft)*
Vertical Obstacle:	*1.1m (3.6ft)*
Trench:	*2.8m (9.18ft)*
Gradient:	*60 percent*
Powerplant:	*Model V-6R diesel*
Power Rating:	*280hp*
Speed – Maximum:	*50km/h (31.25mph)*
Cruising Range:	*450km (281 miles)*
Main Armament:	*4 x 23mm*
Secondary Armament:	*none*
Ammunition:	*2000 x 23mm*

TYPE 88K1

The South Korean Type 88K1 main battle tank, which was developed indigenously, is manufactured in Korea by Hyundai Precision using major components from several different countries. Ssangyong Heavy Industries' military diesel engines for the tank are manufactured under licence from MTU of Germany. In May 1996, Hughes Aircraft Company awarded a contract to Kuchera Defence Systems to manufacture electronic assemblies for programmes for the Korean K1 Tank programme. Deliveries of the 105mm K1 to the South Korean Army were completed in 1997. Hyundai has also undertaken the development of the K1 Armoured Recovery Vehicle and Armoured Vehicle Launched Bridge, both based on the K-1 main battle tank. In 1997 Malaysia announced a plan to purchase about 210 tanks worth $730 million US by the end of the century. The first K1A1 tank with the 120mm main armament rolled off the production line at Hyundai on 3 April 1996. The K1A1 features various enhanced functions compared to the existing K1 tanks, including a primary armament of double the penetration power. The new tank's 120mm gun can penetrate vehicles with armour up to 600mm (23.62in) thick, while the old model's 105mm gun could only penetrate up to 300mm (11.81in) of armour.

SPECIFICATIONS

Type:	main battle tank
Crew:	4
Weight:	51,000kg (112,200lb)
Length (Gun Forward):	9.67m (31.72ft)
Height:	2.24m (7.38ft)
Width:	3.59m (11.77ft)
Ground Clearance:	0.46m (1.5ft)
Vertical Obstacle:	1m (3.28ft)
Trench:	2.74m (8.98ft)
Gradient:	60 percent
Powerplant:	MTU MT 871 Ka 501 diesel
Power Rating:	1200hp
Speed – Maximum:	65km/h (40.62mph)
Cruising Range:	500km (312 miles)
Main Armament:	1 x 105mm
Secondary Armament:	1 x 7.62mm, 1 x 12.7mm
Ammunition:	47 x 105mm, 8800 x 7.62mm

ASCOD

This infantry fighting vehicle is operational with the Spanish Army where it is called the *Pizarro*. The vehicle's main armament is a 30mm dual-feed, gas-operated Mauser Mk 30-2 automatic cannon with a 7.62mm coaxial machine gun as a secondary armament. The 30mm gun has a rate of fire of 800 rounds per minute and can fire a range of ammunition including armour-piercing, fin-stabilized, discarding sabot (APFSDS) rounds. The vehicle carries 200 rounds of 30mm and 700 rounds of 7.62mm ammunition ready to fire, and a store of up to 205 rounds of 30mm and up to 2200 rounds of 7.62mm ammunition. The Ascod has a digital ballistic fire control computer, which can be programmed for up to six ammunition types: five for the 30mm gun and one for the machine gun. The gunner's station is equipped with a Kollsman Day Night Range Sight (DNRS), which has a day channel and thermal imaging sight with an integrated laser rangefinder. The 8 to 12 micron thermal imager is dual field of view and has magnifications of times 2.8 and times 8.4. Two sets of three smoke grenade launchers are installed on each side of the turret. Ascod fighting vehicles can be fitted with a laser warning system and NBC (nuclear, biological, chemical) detection system. The Ascod is an excellent infantry fighting vehicle.

SPECIFICATIONS

Type:	*infantry fighting vehicle*
Crew:	*3 + 8*
Weight:	*25,200kg (55,440lb)*
Length:	*6.83m (22.4ft)*
Height:	*2.65m (8.69ft)*
Width:	*3.15m (10.33ft)*
Ground Clearance:	*0.45m (1.47ft)*
Vertical Obstacle:	*0.95m (3.11ft)*
Trench:	*2.3m (7.54ft)*
Gradient:	*75 percent*
Powerplant:	*MTU 8V-183-TE22 8-V90 diesel*
Power Rating:	*600hp*
Speed – Maximum:	*70km/h (43.75mph)*
Cruising Range:	*500km (312 miles)*
Main Armament:	*1 x 30mm*
Secondary Armament:	*1 x 7.62mm*
Ammunition:	*405 x 30mm, 2900 x 7.62mm*

LT 105 LIGHT TANK

The LT 105 Light Tank has been selected by the Royal Thai Marine Corps, which requires 15 tanks plus one command and one recovery vehicle. It is fitted with a three-man turret such as the 105 Low Recoil Force Turret by Otobreda, or the General Dynamics Low Profile Turret. Main armament is a 105mm semi-automatic low recoil tank gun with a 7.62mm coaxial machine gun. The hull and turret are constructed from all-welded steel armour which provides protection against 14.5mm armour-piercing incendiary rounds over the forward 60-degree arc and all-round protection against 7.62mm weapon attack. Additional ballistic protection is available against APFDS (armour-piercing, fin-stabilized, discarding sabot) rounds up to 30mm in diameter fired from a 1000m (3281ft) range over the forward 60-degree arc, and all-round protection against 14.5mm armour-piercing incendiary (API) rounds from a range of 500m (1640ft). Two sets of three smoke grenade launchers are installed on each side of the turret. Ascod fighting vehicles can be fitted with a laser warning system and NBC (nuclear, biological, chemical) detection system. The Ascod is fitted with an MTU 8V-183-TE22 8-V90 diesel engine, rated at 600hp, and a Renk HSWL 106C hydromechanical transmission, plus torsion bar suspension.

SPECIFICATIONS

Type:	light tank
Crew:	4
Weight:	28,500kg (62,700lb)
Length (Gun Forward):	7.63m (25.03ft)
Height:	2.76m (9.05ft)
Width:	3.15m (10.33ft)
Ground Clearance:	0.45m (1.47ft)
Vertical Obstacle:	0.95m (3.11ft)
Trench:	2.3m (7.54ft)
Gradient:	75 percent
Powerplant:	MTU 8V-183-TE22 8-V90 diesel
Power Rating:	600hp
Speed – Maximum:	70km/h (43.75mph)
Cruising Range:	500km (312 miles)
Main Armament:	1 x 105mm
Secondary Armament:	1 x 7.62mm
Ammunition:	40 x 105mm, 4600 x 7.62mm

STRIDSVAGN 122

The Leopard 2 improved 122 is currently the world's most modern main battle tank (MBT). MBT 122, also known as Leopard 2(S), is a further development of the MBT 121 and is partly manufactured in Sweden. It is the most advanced of the Leopard 2 family of tanks. Deliveries of MBT 122 were commenced in 1997 and completed in 2001. A total of 120 MBTs were delivered. The MBT 122 has a crew of four and armament consists of a 120mm smoothbore gun and two 7.62mm machine guns. The vehicle has night-vision sights for both commander and gunner. Types of ammunition include armour-piercing, fin-stabilized, discarding sabot (APFSDS) and HE (high-explosive) rounds. The vehicle has an eye-proof laser and the fire control system allows firing up to ranges of 4km (2.5 miles). The vehicle has an advanced command/control (C2) system, which comprises radio and intercom (Combat Radio, Type RA 180 for speech/computerized data, plus the LTS 90), a technical terminal for the commander, a display unit for the driver, a navigation system (POS 4) and a vehicle computer. The C2 system offers possibilities of presenting a map with tactical information, target designation, logistic and ballistic information, plus navigational data. Information transfer from one vehicle to another is carried out digitally.

SPECIFICATIONS

Type:	main battle tank
Crew:	4
Weight:	62,000kg (136,400lb)
Length (Gun Forward):	9.74m (31.95ft)
Height:	3m (9.84ft)
Width:	3.81m (12.5ft)
Ground Clearance:	0.54m (1.77ft)
Vertical Obstacle:	1.1m (3.6ft)
Trench:	3m (9.84ft)
Gradient:	60 percent
Powerplant:	MTU MB 873 Ka 501
Power Rating:	1500hp
Speed – Maximum:	72km/h (45mph)
Cruising Range:	500km (312 miles)
Main Armament:	1 x 120mm
Secondary Armament:	2 x 7.62mm
Ammunition:	42 x 120mm, 4750 x 7.62mm

AAVP7A1

The AAVP7A1 is an armoured, amphibious fully tracked landing vehicle. The vehicle carries troops in water operations from ship to shore, through rough water and surf zone. It also carries troops to inland objectives after ashore. The primary responsibility of the amphibious assault vehicles (AAVs) during an amphibious operation is to spearhead a beach assault. Once the AAVs have landed, they can take on several different tasks: manning check points, military operations in urban terrain (MOUT) missions, escorting food convoys or mechanized patrol. The standard AAV comes equipped with a Mk 19 grenade launcher and a M2 0.5in-calibre machine gun. With a 4545kg (10,000lb) capacity, the AAV can also be used as a bulk refueler or a field expedient ambulance. It is easily the most versatile vehicle in the US Marine Corps. When fully combat loaded, and with a three-man crew, it can carry 25 US Marines. In 1985 the Marine Corps changed the designation of the LVTP7Al to AAVP7A1 – amphibious assault vehicle – representing a shift in emphasis away from the long-time LVT designation, meaning Landing Vehicle, Tracked. Without a change of any kind, the AAVP7A1 was to be more of an armoured personnel carrier and less of a landing vehicle and thus more flexible.

SPECIFICATIONS

Type:	armoured personnel carrier
Crew:	3 + 25
Weight:	27,616kg (60,756lb)
Length:	9.04m (29.65ft)
Height:	2.92m (9.58ft)
Width:	3.56m (11.67ft)
Ground Clearance:	0.45m (1.47ft)
Vertical Obstacle:	0.91m (2.98ft)
Trench:	3.65m (11.97ft)
Gradient:	70 percent
Powerplant:	Cummins VT400 turbocharged
Power Rating:	810hp
Speed – Maximum:	48.28km/h (30.17mph)
Cruising Range:	480km (300 miles)
Main Armament:	1 x 12.7mm
Secondary Armament:	none
Ammunition:	2000 x 12.7mm

M1A1

The M1A1 is an improved version of the M1 main battle tank. It includes a 120mm smoothbore main gun, an NBC (nuclear, biological, chemical) overpressure protection system, and an improved armour package. The primary armour-defeating ammunition of the M256 120mm gun is the armour-piercing, fin-stabilized, discarding sabot (APFSDS) round, which features a depleted uranium penetrator. Depleted uranium has a density two and a half times greater than steel and provides high penetration characteristics. Several other types of ammunition are available as well. The gun is reliable, deadly accurate and has a "hit/kill ratio" that equals or surpasses any tank armament in the world. The turret is fitted with two six-barrelled M250 smoke grenade launchers. The standard smoke grenade contains a phosphorus compound that masks thermal signature of the vehicle to the enemy. The stowage for the main armament ammunition is in armoured ammunition boxes behind sliding armour doors. Armour bulkheads separate the crew compartment from the fuel tanks. The tank is equipped with an automatic Halon fire extinguishing system. This system automatically activates within two milliseconds of either a flash or fire within the tank. The top panels of the tank are designed to blow outwards in the event of penetration by a HEAT projectile.

SPECIFICATIONS

Type:	main battle tank
Crew:	4
Weight:	57,141kg (125,710lb)
Length (Gun Forward):	9.76m (32.04ft)
Height:	2.88m (9.46ft)
Width:	3.65m (11.98ft)
Ground Clearance:	0.48m (1.58ft)
Vertical Obstacle:	1.24m (4.08ft)
Trench:	2.74m (9ft)
Gradient:	60 percent
Powerplant:	AGT-1500 gas turbine
Power Rating:	1500hp
Speed – Maximum:	72.42km/h (45.26mph)
Cruising Range:	440km (275 miles)
Main Armament:	1 x 120mm
Secondary Armament:	2 x 7.62mm, 1 x 12.7mm
Ammunition:	55 x 120mm, 11,400 x 7.62mm

M1A2

The M1A2 System Enhanced Program (SEP) is an upgrade to the computer core that is the essence of the M1A2 tank. The SEP upgrade includes improved processors, colour and high-resolution flat panel displays, increased memory capacity, user-friendly Soldier Machine Interface (SMI) and an open operating system that will allow for future growth. Major improvements include the integration of the second-generation forward-looking infrared (FLIR) sight, the Under Armor Auxiliary Power Unit (UAAPU) and a Thermal Management System (TMS). The second-generation FLIR is a fully integrated engagement-sighting system designed to provide the gunner and tank commander with significantly improved day and night target acquisition and engagement capability. This system allows 70 percent better acquisition, 45 percent quicker firing and greater accuracy. In addition, a gain of 30 percent greater range for target acquisition and identification will increase lethality and lessen fratricide. The commander's independent thermal viewer provides a hunter/killer capability. The changes are intended to improve lethality, survivability, mobility, sustainability and to provide increased situational awareness and command and control enhancements necessary to supply information to friendly forces.

SPECIFICATIONS

Type:	*main battle tank*
Crew:	*4*
Weight:	*63,072kg (138,758lb)*
Length (Gun Forward):	*9.76m (32.04ft)*
Height:	*2.88m (9.46ft)*
Width:	*3.65m (11.98ft)*
Ground Clearance:	*0.48m (1.58ft)*
Vertical Obstacle:	*1.24m (4.08ft)*
Trench:	*2.74m (9ft)*
Gradient:	*60 percent*
Powerplant:	*AGT-1500 gas turbine*
Power Rating:	*1500hp*
Speed – Maximum:	*72.42km/h (45.26mph)*
Cruising Range:	*424km (265 miles)*
Main Armament:	*1 x 120mm*
Secondary Armament:	*2 x 7.62mm, 1 x 12.7mm*
Ammunition:	*55 x 120mm, 11,400 x 7.62mm*

M2 BRADLEY

The role of the M2 infantry fighting vehicle is to transport infantry on the battlefield, to provide fire cover to dismounted troops and to suppress enemy tanks and fighting vehicles. The M2 carries three crew – commander, gunner and driver – plus six fully equipped infantrymen. The main armament is a Boeing 25mm M242 Bushmaster chain gun. The M242 has a single barrel with an integrated dual-feed mechanism and remote feed selection. The gunner can select single or multiple shot mode. The standard rate of fire is 200 rounds per minute but the gun is optionally converted to 500 rounds per minute. An M240C 7.62mm machine gun is mounted coaxially to the right of the Bushmaster. The M2 Bradley is also equipped with the Raytheon tube-launched, optically tracked, wire-guided (TOW) BGM-71 anti-tank missile system. The twin-tube TOW launcher is mounted on the left of the turret. The target is tracked using an optical sight which detects the infrared signal from the back of the missile in flight. A double-wire command link between the missile and the gunner is dispensed from two spools at the back of the missile. The launcher sends flight correction data to the guidance system on the missile via the command link. The range of the TOW missile is 3.75km (2.34 miles).

SPECIFICATIONS

Type:	*infantry fighting vehicle*
Crew:	*3 + 6*
Weight:	*22,727kg (50,000lb)*
Length:	*6.55m (21.48ft)*
Height:	*2.97m (9.74ft)*
Width:	*3.61m (11.84ft)*
Ground Clearance:	*0.43m (1.41ft)*
Vertical Obstacle:	*0.91m (2.98ft)*
Trench:	*2.54m (8.33ft)*
Gradient:	*60 percent*
Powerplant:	*Cummins VTA-903T diesel*
Power Rating:	*500hp*
Speed – Maximum:	*66km/h (41.25mph)*
Cruising Range:	*483km (300 miles)*
Main Armament:	*1 x 25mm*
Secondary Armament:	*1 x 7.62mm, 2 x TOW*
Ammunition:	*900 x 25mm, 2200 x 7.62mm*

M3 BRADLEY

The M3 performs scout missions and carries three crew plus two scouts. The Bradley upgrade programme includes improvements based on operational experience in the 1991 Gulf War. The first low-rate initial production M2A3/M3A3 Bradley was delivered in November 1998 and entered service in April 2000. The system was approved for full-rate production in May 2001 (926 Bradley vehicles are to be upgraded). The US Army has ordered two A3 FIST fire support team vehicles, which can conduct digital fire support coordination, laser designation of targets when stationary and target acquisition when on the move. Upgraded target acquisition, automatic and dual target tracking and automated boresighting are being installed. The gunner is equipped with an integrated sight unit (ISU) which includes a day/thermal sight of magnification times 4 and times 12. An optical relay provides the image of the gunner's sight to the commander. The gunner also has periscopes for forward and side observation. The hull of the Bradley is constructed of welded aluminium and spaced laminate armour. In addition, the M2/M3 Bradleys have appliqué steel armour with provision for additional passive armour or explosive reactive armour (ERA) for increased protection against ballistic weapons on the battlefield.

SPECIFICATIONS

Type:	infantry fighting vehicle
Crew:	3 + 2
Weight:	22,727kg (50,000lb)
Length:	6.55m (21.48ft)
Height:	2.97m (9.74ft)
Width:	3.61m (11.84ft)
Ground Clearance:	0.43m (1.41ft)
Vertical Obstacle:	0.91m (2.98ft)
Trench:	2.54m (8.33ft)
Gradient:	60 percent
Powerplant:	Cummins VTA-903T diesel
Power Rating:	500hp
Speed – Maximum:	66km/h (41.25mph)
Cruising Range:	483km (300 miles)
Main Armament:	1 x 25mm
Secondary Armament:	1 x 7.62mm, 2 x TOW
Ammunition:	900 x 25mm, 2200 x 7.62mm

M6 BRADLEY LINEBACKER

The Linebacker's combined-arms mission is to provide air defence protection to forward area heavy manoeuvre combat forces, combat support elements, and other critical friendly assets from attack by enemy rotary wing, fixed-wing, unmanned aerial vehicles and cruise missiles. The Bradley Linebacker consists of the M2A2(ODS) Bradley with an integrated, externally mounted launcher that can fire four Stinger missiles while stationary or on the move. An integrated position, navigation and north-seeker capability allows for on-the-move cueing. The standard vehicle-mounted launcher (SVML) carrying four Stinger missiles is added to the 25mm gun turret, eliminating the tube-launched, optically-tracked, wired-guided (TOW) missile which is standard to the Bradley. The 25mm chain gun contributes to the air defence firepower and, as with the 7.62mm machine gun, also provides self-defence. In the event of launcher system damage or failure, or should the manoeuvre force commander choose to employ the Linebacker in a static mode, the system maintains a dismounted Stinger missile capability. Bradley Linebacker retains the capability to maintain pace with the armoured force. Six Stinger missiles are carried internally as ammunition for the external launcher.

SPECIFICATIONS

Type:	air defence vehicle
Crew:	5
Weight:	22,727kg (50,000lb)
Length:	6.55m (21.48ft)
Height:	2.97m (9.74ft)
Width:	3.61m (11.84ft)
Ground Clearance:	0.43m (1.41ft)
Vertical Obstacle:	0.91m (2.98ft)
Trench:	2.54m (8.33ft)
Gradient:	60 percent
Powerplant:	Cummins VTA-903T diesel
Power Rating:	500hp
Speed – Maximum:	66km/h (41.25mph)
Cruising Range:	450km (281 miles)
Main Armament:	1 x 25mm cannon
Secondary Armament:	1 x 7.62mm, 4 x Stinger SAM
Ammunition:	300 x 25mm, 2800 x 7.62mm

M44

Although the M44 155mm Self-propelled Gun has been withdrawn from service with the US Army after seeing service in the Korean and Vietnam Wars, it is still operated by a number of other allied countries, including Turkey. The upgraded M44T system has increased mobility, firepower and reliability. The M44T upgrade package was originally developed in the late 1980s by a German consortium of GLS, MTU and Rheinmetall. The latter company was responsible for the ordnance which is similar to that used on the upgraded M109A3G of the German Army, which in turn is based on that used in the towed FH-70 system. Turkey has modernized its old US-built 155mm M44 guns in a number of key areas, including the installation of a 155mm 39-calibre ordnance and the replacement of the petrol engine by a more fuel-efficient German MTU MB 833 Aa 501 diesel engine developing 450hp, coupled to the original Allison automatic transmission. The original M44 fired a high-explosive projectile to a maximum range of 14.6km (9.12 miles), while the upgraded M44T has a maximum range of 24.7km (15.43 miles) using standard ammunition or 30km (18.75 miles) using enhanced projectiles. The M44 will remain in service around the world well into this century.

SPECIFICATIONS

Type:	*self-propelled gun*
Crew:	*5*
Weight:	*28,350kg (62,370lb)*
Length (Gun Forward):	*6.15m (spade up) (20.17ft)*
Height:	*3.11m (10.2ft)*
Width:	*3.23m (10.59ft)*
Ground Clearance:	*0.48m (1.57ft)*
Vertical Obstacle:	*0.76m (2.49ft)*
Trench:	*1.82m (5.97ft)*
Gradient:	*60 percent*
Powerplant:	*MTU MB 833 Aa 501 diesel*
Power Rating:	*450hp*
Speed – Maximum:	*56km/h (35mph)*
Cruising Range:	*122km (76.25 miles)*
Main Armament:	*1 x 155mm*
Secondary Armament:	*1 x 12.7mm*
Ammunition:	*24 x 155mm, 900 x 12.7mm*

M48A5

Developed from the M47 "General Patton" tank, the M48 was the mainstay of the US Army and Marines in Vietnam. Some 11,703 M48s were built between 1952 and 1959. Originally they had 90mm guns, but upon modification to the M48A5 standard they were given the British 105mm. The M48 was withdrawn from US service in favour of the M60, a further development of the M48, but the M48 Patton remains in service around the world. The M48 vehicle is separated into three compartments: the driver's compartment, the fighting compartment and the engine compartment. Above the main gun is a one-million candle-power Xenon searchlight. This light has both a white light and an infrared mode. It is boresighted with the main gun and gunsights so that it can be used to illuminate a target at night. There are a number of variants: M48A5K, South Korean variant with 105mm gun and improved fire control system; M48A5E, Spanish variant with 105mm gun and laser rangefinder; M48A5T1, Turkish upgrade, similar to M48A5; T2 variant includes a thermal sight; CM11, Taiwan variant with a modified M48H turret mated to the M60 hull; CM12, Taiwan variant mates the CM11 turret to the existing M48A3 hull; and M67 flamethrower with a shorter, thicker barrel than the normal 90mm-armed version.

SPECIFICATIONS

Type:	main battle tank
Crew:	4
Weight:	48,089kg (107,595lb)
Length (Gun Forward):	9.29m (30.5ft)
Height:	3.08m (10.1ft)
Width:	3.63m (11.9ft)
Ground Clearance:	0.41m (1.34ft)
Vertical Obstacle:	0.91m (2.98ft)
Trench:	2.59m (8.49ft)
Gradient:	60 percent
Powerplant:	AVDS-1790-2D diesel
Power Rating:	690hp
Speed – Maximum:	48km/h (30mph)
Cruising Range:	413km (258 miles)
Main Armament:	1 x 105mm
Secondary Armament:	1 x 7.62mm, 1 x 12.7mm
Ammunition:	54 x 105mm, 10,000 x 7.62mm

M60

The M60 is one of the world's most successful main battle tanks, with 15,000 having been produced and serving in the armies of 22 countries. The main gun is the 105mm M68 rifled gun with 63 rounds of ammunition. The gun is fully stabilized in the elevation and traverse axes, and is fitted with a thermal sleeve. Both gunner and commander are able to fire the gun and select the type of ammunition to be fired. The coaxial weapon is the 7.62mm M240 machine gun. The tank has two smoke generation systems: an engine exhaust smoke system which sprays fuel into the exhaust manifold, and two six-barrelled smoke grenade launchers which are fitted on ether side of the turret. The tank is fitted with a Raytheon fire control system including an AN/WG-2 eye-safe laser rangefinder and M21 ballistic computer. The gunner's sight is boresighted with the laser rangefinder and the tank's M21 fire control computer senses the type of ammunition which has been selected. The gunner provides the input data for the air temperature and pressure. Other input data is downloaded from various sensors: the target range from the laser rangefinder and cant, crosswind and inertial tracking rates from the gun stabilization unit. This allows accurate engagement against moving targets while the tank is on the move.

SPECIFICATIONS

Type:	main battle tank
Crew:	4
Weight:	52,617kg (115,757lb)
Length (Gun Forward):	9.43m (30.95ft)
Height:	3.27m (10.72ft)
Width:	3.63m (11.9ft)
Ground Clearance:	0.45m (1.47ft)
Vertical Obstacle:	0.91m (2.98ft)
Trench:	2.59m (8.49ft)
Gradient:	60 percent
Powerplant:	AVDS-1790-2C diesel
Power Rating:	750hp
Speed – Maximum:	48km/h (30mph)
Cruising Range:	480km (300 miles)
Main Armament:	1 x 105mm
Secondary Armament:	1 x 7.62mm, 1 x 12.7mm
Ammunition:	63 x 105mm, 7000 x 12.7 & 7.62mm

M109

The 155mm M109 self-propelled medium howitzer is a highly mobile combat support weapon that first saw service in the early 1960s. It has a cruising range of 349km (218 miles) at speeds up to 56.3km/h (35mph). The M109A2/A3/A4 howitzers use the M185 cannon and achieve a range of 23.5km (14.68 miles). The replacement of the 23-calibre barrel with the M284 cannon 39-calibre barrel on the M109A5/A6 increases the range capability to 30km (18.75 miles). The 155mm projectile weighs 44.54kg (98lb). The howitzer is a vehicle that provides armoured combat support, is air transportable, internally loaded, and has excellent ground mobility. It allows firing in a 360-degree circle through its primary armament, the 155mm gun, and its secondary armament, the M2 heavy machine gun. The system is capable of both direct (line of sight) and indirect (out of the line of sight) firing. On 24 May 2000, the government of Egypt requested a possible sale of 279 M109A2/A3 155mm self-propelled howitzers, support equipment, spare and repair parts, publications and technical data, personnel training and training equipment, US government and contractor engineering and logistics personnel services, and other related elements of logistics support. The estimated cost was $48 million US.

SPECIFICATIONS

Type:	self-propelled howitzer
Crew:	6
Weight:	24,948kg (54,886lb)
Length (Gun Forward):	9.12m (29.92ft)
Height:	3m (9.84ft)
Width:	3.15m (10.33ft)
Ground Clearance:	0.45m (1.47ft)
Vertical Obstacle:	0.53m (1.73ft)
Trench:	1.83m (6ft)
Gradient:	60 percent
Powerplant:	Detroit Diesel Model 8V-711
Power Rating:	405hp
Speed – Maximum:	56.3km/h (35mph)
Cruising Range:	349km (218 miles)
Main Armament:	1 x 155mm howitzer
Secondary Armament:	1 x 12.7mm
Ammunition:	36 x 155mm, 500 x 12.7mm

M109A6 PALADIN

The M109A6 Paladin is the latest advancement in 155mm self-propelled artillery. The system enhances previous versions of the M109 by implementing onboard navigational and automatic fire control systems. Paladin has both a Kevlar-lined chassis and a pressurized crew compartment to guard against ballistic, nuclear, biological and chemical threats. The M109A6 is the most technologically advanced cannon in the US Army inventory, has a four-man crew and has a cruising range of 298km (186 miles). The Paladin can operate independently, on the move, it can receive a fire mission, compute firing data, select and take up its firing position, automatically unlock and point its cannon, fire and move out, all with no external technical assistance. Firing the first round from the move in under 60 seconds, a "shoot and scoot" capability protects the crew from counter-battery fire. The M109A6 Paladin is capable of firing up to four rounds per minute to ranges of 30km (18.75 miles). The Paladin features increased survivability characteristics such as day/night operability, NBC (nuclear, biological, chemical) protection with climate control and secure voice and digital communications. The crew remains in the vehicle throughout the mission. The US requirement for these vehicles is estimated to be more than 2000.

SPECIFICATIONS

Type:	self-propelled gun
Crew:	4
Weight:	28,909kg (63,600lb)
Length (Gun Forward):	9.12m (29.92ft)
Height:	3m (9.84ft)
Width:	3.15m (10.33ft)
Ground Clearance:	0.45m (1.47ft)
Vertical Obstacle:	0.53m (1.73ft)
Trench:	1.83m (6ft)
Gradient:	60 percent
Powerplant:	Detroit Diesel DDEC 8V71T
Power Rating:	440hp
Speed – Maximum:	56.3km/h (35mph)
Cruising Range:	298km (186 miles)
Main Armament:	1 x 155mm
Secondary Armament:	1 x 12.7mm
Ammunition:	39 x 155mm, 500 x 12.7mm

M110A2

The M110A2 is a self-propelled heavy artillery cannon with a crew of 12. Designed to be part of a common family of weapons utilizing the same chassis components, the M107 and M110 were essentially the same vehicle mounting different barrels. This fully tracked, self-propelled artillery weapon fires a 90.9kg (200lb) projectile 203mm (8in) in diameter. The shell leaves the muzzle at a velocity of 700 metres per second (2300 feet per second) and can travel more than 28.8km (18 miles). Ammunition includes standard high explosives, bomblets and high-explosive rockets. The M115 gun has a stepped thread/interrupted screw breechblock, a hydropneumatic variable recoil mechanism and a pneumatic equilibrator. This howitzer system was designed to provide medium-range, general support artillery fire. The M110A2 was built by Bowen-McLauchlin-York of York, Pennsylvania. Widely used in Vietnam, the US Army received this howitzer in 1963 and it served for nearly 30 years. There were 1023 M110A2s in the army inventory in the early 1990s, prior to the system being phased out of service. However, it is still in service with other armies around the world: Belgium, Denmark, Greece, India, Japan, Jordan, South Korea, Spain and Taiwan. It is still deployed with US National Guard units.

SPECIFICATIONS

Type:	*self-propelled gun*
Crew:	*12*
Weight:	*26,534kg (58,374lb)*
Length (Gun Forward):	*10.73m (35.2ft)*
Height:	*3.14m (10.33ft)*
Width:	*3.14m (10.33ft)*
Ground Clearance:	*0.44m (1.44ft)*
Vertical Obstacle:	*1.01m (3.31ft)*
Trench:	*2.36m (7.74ft)*
Gradient:	*60 percent*
Powerplant:	*Detroit Diesel Model 8V-71T*
Power Rating:	*405hp*
Speed – Maximum:	*56km/h (35mph)*
Cruising Range:	*725km (453 miles)*
Main Armament:	*1 x 203mm*
Secondary Armament:	*none*
Ammunition:	*2 x 203mm*

M113

The M113 armoured personnel carrier (APC) was the first modern "battle taxi" developed to transport infantry forces on the mechanized battlefield. It is fitted with a two-stroke six-cylinder Detroit diesel providing power through a three-speed automatic gearbox and steering differential. The M113 is built of aircraft-quality aluminum which allows it to possess some of the same strengths as steel at a much lighter weight. This distinct weight advantage allows the M113 to utilize a relatively small engine to power the vehicle, as well as carry a large payload cross-country. Since their initial introduction in 1960, M113-based systems have entered service in more than 50 countries. The systems have been modified into more than 40 identified specific variants, with many times that number of minor field modifications. Many of these modifications have been developed by foreign governments to meet their specific national requirements. Today's M113 fleet includes about 4000 M113A3 vehicles equipped with the most recent recent A3 RISE (Reliability Improvements for Selected Equipment) package. The standard RISE package includes an upgraded propulsion system, greatly improved driver controls (new power brakes and conventional steering controls), external fuel tanks, and 200-amp alternator with four batteries.

SPECIFICATIONS

Type:	*armoured personnel carrier*
Crew:	*2 + 11*
Weight:	*12,272kg (27,000lb)*
Length:	*4.86m (15.95ft)*
Height:	*2.19m (7.2ft)*
Width:	*2.68m (8.79ft)*
Ground Clearance:	*0.43m (1.41ft)*
Vertical Obstacle:	*0.61m (2ft)*
Trench:	*1.68m (5.51ft)*
Gradient:	*60 percent*
Powerplant:	*Detroit Diesel Model 6V-53T*
Power Rating:	*212hp*
Speed – Maximum:	*60.7km/h (37mph)*
Cruising Range:	*480km (300 miles)*
Main Armament:	*1 x 12.7mm*
Secondary Armament:	*none*
Ammunition:	*2000 x 12.7mm*

M270 MLRS

The Multiple Launch Rocket System (MLRS) provides an all-weather, indirect area fire weapon system to attack counter-battery, air defence, armoured formations and other high-priority targets at all depths of the tactical battlefield. Primary missions of MLRS include the suppression, neutralization and destruction of threat fire support and forward area air defence targets. The Multiple Launch Rocket System is a versatile weapon system that supplements traditional cannon artillery fire by delivering large volumes of firepower in a short time against critical, time-sensitive targets. MLRS units can use their system's "shoot and scoot" capability to survive while providing fire support for attacking manoeuvre elements. MLRS is not intended to replace cannon artillery, but has been designed to complement it. MLRS consists of a self-loading launcher with an onboard fire control system (FCS). The launcher is mounted on a mobile track vehicle that carries 12 rockets or two Army Tactical Missile System (ATACMS) missiles, which can be fired individually or simultaneously. Rockets have a range beyond 30km (18.75 miles), and the US Army TACMS Block IA missile can reach to 300km (187.5 miles). A conventional barrage of 12 rockets delivers 7728 bomblets or 336 scatterable mines.

SPECIFICATIONS

Type:	multiple rocket launcher
Crew:	3
Weight:	25,000kg (55,000lb)
Length:	6.88m (22.6ft)
Height:	2.57m (8.43ft)
Width:	2.97m (9.75ft)
Ground Clearance:	0.43m (1.41ft)
Vertical Obstacle:	1m (3.28ft)
Trench:	2.29m (7.51ft)
Gradient:	60 percent
Powerplant:	Cummins VTA-903T diesel
Power Rating:	500hp
Speed – Maximum:	64km/h (40mph)
Cruising Range:	483km (302 miles)
Main Armament:	12 x 227mm rockets
Secondary Armament:	none
Ammunition:	none

M270A1 MLRS

The MLRS M270 launcher is being upgraded to accommodate a new MLRS family of munitions, including the US Army Tactical Missile System. The improvements provided by the M270A1 will enhance the field artillery's support to armour and infantry units. They will reinforce the dominant manoeuvre force by improving the corps commander's precision engagement capabilities for shaping the battlefield at extended ranges. The Improved Fire Control System (IFCS) replaces obsolete, maintenance-intensive hardware and software, providing growth potential for future munitions and the possibility of reduced launcher operation and support costs. A Global Positioning System-aided navigation system for the launcher is being developed as part of IFCS to supplement the existing inertial position-navigation system. The Improved Launcher Mechanical System (ILMS) is designed to decrease the time required to aim and load the launcher. This is achieved by providing a faster launcher drive system that moves simultaneously in azimuth and elevation. ILMS is expected to reduce the traverse time from the stowed position to worst case aim point by 80 percent. It will also decrease the mechanical system contribution to reload time by about 40 percent. Reduced launch and reload time will increase survivability.

SPECIFICATIONS

Type:	multiple rocket launcher
Crew:	3
Weight:	25,000kg (55,000lb)
Length:	6.88m (22.6ft)
Height:	2.57m (8.43ft)
Width:	2.97m (9.75ft)
Ground Clearance:	0.43m (1.41ft)
Vertical Obstacle:	1m (3.28ft)
Trench:	2.29m (7.51ft)
Gradient:	60 percent
Powerplant:	Cummings VTA-903T diesel
Power Rating:	500hp
Speed – Maximum:	64km/h (40mph)
Cruising Range:	483km (302 miles)
Main Armament:	12 x 227mm rockets
Secondary Armament:	none
Ammunition:	none

M551 SHERIDAN

The M551 Sheridan was developed to provide the US Army with a light armoured reconnaissance vehicle with heavy firepower. The main armament consists of an 152mm M81 gun/missile launcher capable of firing conventional ammunition and the MGM-51 Shillelagh anti-tank missile. Due to problems with the gun-tube-launched anti-tank missile, the Sheridan was not fielded widely throughout the army. The gun would foul with caseless ammunition, gun firing would interfere with missile electronics, and the entire vehicle recoiled with unusual vigour when the gun was fired, since the 152mm gun was too big for the light-weight chassis. The Shillelagh missiles were evidently never used in anger. In addition to the main gun/missile launcher, the M551 is armed with a 7.62mm M240 machine gun and a 12.7mm M2 anti-aircraft machine gun. Protection for the four-man crew is provided by an aluminum hull and steel turret. Although light enough to be airdropped, the aluminum armour is thin enough to be pierced by heavy machine-gun rounds, and the vehicle is particularly vulnerable to mines. As projectile technology advanced, the Sheridan's potential declined and it was phased out of the US inventory beginning in 1978. However, the M551 is still used by the 82nd Airborne Division.

SPECIFICATIONS

Type:	*light tank*
Crew:	*4*
Weight:	*15,830kg (34,826lb)*
Length:	*6.79m (22.3ft)*
Height:	*2.94m (9.64ft)*
Width:	*4.11m (13.5ft)*
Ground Clearance:	*0.48m (1.57ft)*
Vertical Obstacle:	*0.83m (2.62ft)*
Trench:	*2.54m (8.3ft)*
Gradient:	*60 percent*
Powerplant:	*Detroit Diesel Model 6V-53T*
Power Rating:	*300hp*
Speed – Maximum:	*70km/h (43.75mph)*
Cruising Range:	*600km (375 miles)*
Main Armament:	*1 x 152mm*
Secondary Armament:	*1 x 7.62mm, 1 x 12.7mm*
Ammunition:	*20 x 152mm, 3080 x 7.62mm*

M730 CHAPARRAL

This lightweight carrier is a product improved version of the M730A1 that is used to transport the improved (and heavier) M54A2 Chaparral Aerial Intercept Guided Missile pallet. The vehicle incorporates the Reliability Improvement for Selected Equipment (RISE) power package and a nuclear, biological, chemical (NBC) collective protection system. The M730A2 was the first M113 derivative to use the RISE package. Approximately 500 M730A1 systems were converted to M730A2 RISE during the period 1988–93 at three depot locations. Fieldings were completed in the third quarter of 1993. Residual conversion kits are being used to support M548A1 to M548A3 conversions. The Chaparral missile provides mobile short-range air defence to defeat low-altitude aircraft. The system is designed to be mobile, self-contained and air transportable. The M730 is a mobile light air defence system with a turret mounted on a tracked vehicle carrying four ready-to-fire missiles; the Chaparral is a ground-launched version of the air-to-air Sidewinder. Chaparral consists of infrared heat-seeking missiles, a launcher with a forward-looking infrared (FLIR) sight, and a tracked vehicle. Chaparral provides the US Army with point defence of vital corps areas against direct enemy air attack.

SPECIFICATIONS

Type:	*self-propelled SAM*
Crew:	*4*
Weight:	*11,909kg (26,200lb)*
Length:	*6.04m (19.83ft)*
Height:	*2.89m (9.43ft)*
Width:	*2.68m (8.79ft)*
Ground Clearance:	*0.43m (1.41ft)*
Vertical Obstacle:	*0.61m (2ft)*
Trench:	*1.68m (5.51ft)*
Gradient:	*60 percent*
Powerplant:	*Detroit Diesel Model 6V-53*
Power Rating:	*212hp*
Speed – Maximum:	*60km/h (37.5mph)*
Cruising Range:	*480km (300 miles)*
Main Armament:	*4 x Chaparral SAM*
Secondary Armament:	*none*
Ammunition:	*12 x Chaparral SAM*

M901A3

The M901A3 Improved TOW Vehicle (ITV) is a weapon system using TOW components mounted on a modified M113A3. It incorporates the RISE power-pack and improved driver controls. The TOW components are mounted in a launcher platform that is attached to a modified M27 cupola. An elevating mechanism positions the launcher platform into reload and elevated positions. The system is capable of firing two missiles without reloading and carries 10 TOW rounds in the missile rack. The BGM-71 TOW wire-guided heavy anti-tank missile is used in anti-armour, anti-bunker, anti-fortification and anti-amphibious landing roles. The missile has command to line-of-sight guidance. The weapons operator uses a telescopic sight to view a point on the target and then fires the missile. The missile has a two-stage solid propellant rocket motor. Guidance signals from the guidance computer are transmitted along two wires, which spool from the back of the missile to the control system on the missile. The CACS-2 control system uses differential piston-type actuators. For penetration of tanks protected with explosive reactive armour (ERA), TOW 2A is equipped with a tandem warhead. A small disrupter charge detonates the reactive armour and allows the main shaped charge to penetrate the main armour.

SPECIFICATIONS

Type:	*armoured TOW carrier*
Crew:	*4*
Weight:	*11,794kg (25,947lb)*
Length:	*4.83m (15.84ft)*
Height:	*3.35m (11ft)*
Width:	*2.68m (8.79ft)*
Ground Clearance:	*0.43m (1.41ft)*
Vertical Obstacle:	*0.61m (2ft)*
Trench:	*1.68m (5.51ft)*
Gradient:	*60 percent*
Powerplant:	*Detroit Diesel Model 6V-53T*
Power Rating:	*215hp*
Speed – Maximum:	*67km/h (41.87mph)*
Cruising Range:	*483km (302 miles)*
Main Armament:	*1 x twin TOW ATGW launcher*
Secondary Armament:	*1 x 7.62mm*
Ammunition:	*2 + 10 TOW, 1000 x 7.62mm*

M981 FISTV

The M981 Fire Support Team Vehicle (FISTV) is used as an artillery forward observer vehicle in accordance with the US fire support team concept. Its primary mission is to enhance combined arms efficiency by providing the FIST headquarters with an operating base for targeting, self-locating and designating equipment which will provide improvements in first-round accuracy and by providing mobility and survivability comparable with the manoeuvre units being supported. The weapons station on the M981 contains the AN/TVQ-2 ground and vehicle laser locator designator with north-finding module and line-of-sight sub-system, land navigation system and extensive communications equipment. The turret of the M981 is designed to mimic that of the M901, thus making the vehicle less conspicuous to enemies. The M981 incorporates the armoured external fuel tank system for increased stowage capability and increased crew survivability. The first conversions from M113A2 chassis began in 1983 and the first production vehicles appeared in December 1984. The US Army has a total requirement for 967 FISTVs. First deliveries to US units were made in 1985 and deployments were completed in 1990. The FISTV fitted with the RISE power package is designated the M981A3.

SPECIFICATIONS

Type:	artillery observation vehicle
Crew:	4
Weight:	11,794kg (25,947lb)
Length:	4.83m (15.84ft)
Height:	3.35m (11ft)
Width:	2.68m (8.79ft)
Ground Clearance:	0.43m (1.41ft)
Vertical Obstacle:	0.61m (2ft)
Trench:	1.68m (5.51ft)
Gradient:	60 percent
Powerplant:	Detroit Diesel Model 6V-53T
Power Rating:	215hp
Speed – Maximum:	67km/h (41.87mph)
Cruising Range:	483km (302 miles)
Main Armament:	1 x twin TOW ATGW launcher
Secondary Armament:	1 x 7.62mm
Ammunition:	2 + 10 TOW, 1000 x 7.62mm

M1064A3

The M1064A3 is a member of the M113A3 vehicle family developed and produced by FMC Corporation. Power is supplied by a 275hp Detroit Diesel Model 6V53T turbocharged diesel engine driving through an Allison X200-4 (cross-drive) transmission. The M1064A3 incorporates all of the mobility and reliability improvements of the M113A3 vehicle, including powertrain, engine diagnostics, driver's station, and electrical system. Survivability is enhanced through the use of external fuel tanks. The M1064A3 has the same silhouette as the M113A3 armoured personnel carrier and features a welded-in cross beam, additional floor support structures to withstand mortar reaction forces, and an enlarged three-piece top firing hatch. The 120mm weapon has a 90-degree traverse for firing over the rear of the vehicle. The M106 107mm mortar carrier has a 4.2in (107mm) M30 mortar mounted on a turntable in the rear which fires through a large hatch in the roof. The baseplate for the mortar is mounted externally on the left side of the vehicle for use when firing the mortar dismounted. However, as can be seen from the photograph, the crew is vulnerable to small-arms fire. The M125 vehicle is of similar design, carrying a 81mm mortar. Kits to convert M106 and M125 vehicles to the M1064A3 configuration are available.

SPECIFICATIONS

Type:	self-propelled mortar
Crew:	6
Weight:	12,809kg (28,240lb)
Length:	4.86m (15.94ft)
Height:	2.31m (7.57ft)
Width:	2.68m (8.79ft)
Ground Clearance:	0.43m (1.41ft)
Vertical Obstacle:	0.61m (2ft)
Trench:	1.68m (5.51ft)
Gradient:	60 percent
Powerplant:	Detroit Diesel Model 6V53T
Power Rating:	275hp
Speed – Maximum:	66km/h (41mph)
Cruising Range:	480km (300 miles)
Main Armament:	1 x 120mm mortar
Secondary Armament:	1 x 12.7mm
Ammunition:	69 x 120mm, 2000 x 12.7mm

M2001 CRUSADER

The Crusader self-propelled howitzer is a replacement for the Paladin and the US Army requirement is expected to be for over 800 vehicles, entry into service beginning in 2008. Crusader provides enhanced survivability, lethality and mobility and is more easily deployable and sustainable than current systems. A battery of six Crusaders can deliver 15,000kg (33,000lb) of ammunition in less than five minutes. Crusader consists of two vehicles, the M2001 155mm self-propelled howitzer and the M2002 armoured re-supply vehicle. The 155mm self-propelled howitzer has fully automated ammunition handling and firing that allows firing of the 39 onboard rounds at rates of up to 10 rounds per minute to ranges in excess of 40km (25 miles). The first rounds of a mission can be fired in 15 to 30 seconds. Additionally, one Crusader vehicle can fire up to eight rounds to strike a single target at the same time. The digital fire control system calculates separate firing solutions for each of the eight projectiles. Crusader is re-supplied by the M2002 ammunition re-supply vehicle, which is equipped with a fully automated ammunition handling subsystem. This allows its three-man re-supply crew to automatically transfer, under armour, up to 48 rounds of ammunition and fuel in less than 12 minutes.

SPECIFICATIONS

Type:	self-propelled howitzer
Crew:	3
Weight:	36,100kg (79,420lb)
Length (Gun Forward):	12.89m (42.3ft)
Height:	2.89m (9.5ft)
Width:	3.5m (11.5ft)
Ground Clearance:	0.43m (1.43ft)
Vertical Obstacle:	0.79m (2.6ft)
Trench:	0.82m (2.7ft)
Gradient:	60 percent
Powerplant:	Honeywell LV100-5
Power Rating:	440hp
Speed – Maximum:	67.2km/h (42mph)
Cruising Range:	402km (251 miles)
Main Armament:	1 x 155mm
Secondary Armament:	1 x 12.7mm
Ammunition:	39 x 155, 500 x 12.7mm

MK154

The MK154 Launcher, Mine Clearance (LMC) is part of the Mark 1 Mine Clearance System which also includes three M59 Linear Demolition Charges (LDCs), three MK22 Mod 3/4 Rockets and an AAVP7A1 vehicle. Its role is to breach a lane through a minefield during an amphibious assault and subsequent operations inland. The MK154 LMC can deploy three linear demolition chargers from the water or land. Each linear demolition charge is 100m (328ft) long and will be the initial minefield breaching asset used. Because the LDC is only effective against single impulse, non-blast resistant, pressure-fused mines, a mechanical proofing device must also be used in a lane that has been explosively breached. The MK154 LMC is an electric and hydraulic system which can be installed into any AAVP7A1. All of the hydraulics are self-contained, and the electrical power is provided through the host vehicle slave receptacle. The system has the capability to house and fire three LDCs using three MK22 Rockets. The overpressure created by each of the LDCs will clear a path 16m (52.49ft) wide and 100m (328ft) long through a minefield. The width of the lane and the ability to neutralize mines is dependent upon the mine type and fusing. The MK154 is a valuable asset to the US Marine Corps.

SPECIFICATIONS

Type:	mine clearer
Crew:	3
Weight:	37,442kg (82,372lb)
Length:	9.04m (29.65ft)
Height:	2.92m (9.58ft)
Width:	3.56m (11.67ft)
Ground Clearance:	0.45m (1.47ft)
Vertical Obstacle:	0.91m (2.98ft)
Trench:	3.65m (11.97ft)
Gradient:	70 percent
Powerplant:	Continental LV-1790-1 petrol
Power Rating:	810hp
Speed – Maximum:	48km/h (30mph)
Cruising Range:	480km (300 miles)
Main Armament:	1 x 7.62mm
Secondary Armament:	none
Ammunition:	2000 x 7.62mm

STINGRAY

The Stingray light tank was developed to fill requirements for a light tank with increased strategic and tactical mobility and main battle tank firepower. It was developed with the export market in mind. For example, it fires all NATO 105mm ammunition, as well as British and US armour-piercing, fin-stabilized, discarding sabot (APFSDS) rounds. Stingray can climb 60-percent gradients, and traverses 2.7ft (822mm) vertical obstacles and water depths to 3.5ft (1066mm). The Stingray is the only light tank mounting the NATO 105mm cannon currently in production. Textron Marine & Land Systems has now completed an advanced version of the Stingray, known as Stingray II, which has increased ballistic protection and improved fire control, and is expected to have wide appeal to many international customers. The tank's sensors include an M36E1 SIE day/night sight with laser rangefinder for gunner and optional thermal sight, seven periscopes for commander with optional NV52 day/night sight, and an optional digital fire control system. The tank can be fitted with a nuclear, biological, chemical (NBC) protection system. Other defensive measures include two four-shot smoke grenade dischargers. Secondary armament consists of either two 7.62mm machine guns or one 7.62mm and one 12.7mm.

SPECIFICATIONS

Type:	*light tank*
Crew:	*4*
Weight:	*21,205kg (46,651lb)*
Length (Gun Forward):	*9.30m (30.51ft)*
Height:	*2.55m (8.36ft)*
Width:	*2.71m (8.89ft)*
Ground Clearance:	*0.46m (1.56ft)*
Vertical Obstacle:	*0.82m (2.7ft)*
Trench:	*2.13m (6.98ft)*
Gradient:	*60 percent*
Powerplant:	*Detroit Diesel Model 8V-92TA*
Power Rating:	*535hp*
Speed – Maximum:	*67km/h (42mph)*
Cruising Range:	*483km (302 miles)*
Main Armament:	*1 x 105mm*
Secondary Armament:	*2 x 7.62mm*
Ammunition:	*32 x 105mm, 2800 x 7.62mm*

INDEX